Exposing the Fig Leaf Conspiracy

Barry Perez and Jan Perez
With Bonney Rosas

Edited by Judy Klein

HARVESTIME MINISTRIES INTERNATIONAL
AND B. ROSES PUBLISHING

First Printing 2026

ISBN No. 978-1-971741-00-0

Acknowledgments

I wish to thank Bonney Rosas for her key role in the completion of this book. Her invaluable contributions added depth and insights into my theme and desire of the book, which is to lead readers to a place of decision to follow God's original, intended purpose to display and reveal His glory. Bonney is a gifted vessel of our Lord Jesus Christ and I look forward to all that God will continue to accomplish through her life and ministry both now and the years to come.

I would also like to express my sincere appreciation to Judy Klein for her expertise in editing the book. She and her husband, Bill, have been dear friends for nearly 30 years. She is a committed Christian, a career educator and an avid student of the Bible. Her evaluation of this work is well-received and highly valued.

Table of Contents

Introduction

"Then the eyes of both of them were opened, and they realized they were naked; so they sewed fig leaves together and made coverings for themselves."
Genesis 3:7 (NIV)

This book starts with laying the foundation for the journey that every person makes throughout his or her entire life. All of us can probably identify with the desire to achieve a sense of value and worth. So often this need is expressed through overperforming in our talents, gifts, education, and other accomplishments that we hope will validate us.

You were created to reflect the glory and greatness of God. This can be an unspoken and unrealized inner need that cries out, "You must believe that I have value, I have worth, and that I am somebody. Look at what I can do. Look at what I have done. Look at who I've become."

These things do have a measure of validity; however, they will never bring lasting fulfillment and happiness. They can, and often do, lead to patterns of behavior that damage us and our relationships. How do we become restored?

The Christian philosopher Blaise Pascal said that every person is born with a God-shaped hole that only God can fill. That is, of course, our modern vernacular – Pascal's exact quote was, "…What is it then, that this desire and this inability proclaim to us, but that there was once in man a true happiness of which there now remain to him only the mark and empty trace, which he in vain tries to fill from all his surroundings, seeking from things absent the help he does not obtain in things present? But these are all inadequate, because the infinite abyss can only be filled by an infinite and immutable object, that is to say, only by God Himself." Whether you like to keep it simple or enjoy Pascal's longer speech, the point is clear. We are divinely created, but also fallen and inadequate, grasping at things that never deliver. How did we end up here?

Adam and Eve were covered with the glory of God at creation. In Genesis 3:4-7, Satan came to steal this beautiful covering. By separating them from the Father and promising self-sufficiency, Satan stripped the glory covering from Adam and Eve, leaving them naked and ashamed, so they sewed fig leaves together as a replacement covering to hide their nakedness. And it is in this very condition that many people find themselves today. How can we be restored?

"Then Jesus was led by the Spirit into the wilderness to be tempted by the devil. After fasting forty days and forty nights, he was hungry. The tempter came to him and said, "If you are the Son of God, tell these stones to become bread."
Matthew 4:1-3 (NIV)

2

At Jesus' baptism when Heaven was opened and the Father said, "This is My beloved Son in whom I am well pleased!", the Father gave Jesus His identity. But 40 days later, Satan tempted Jesus to doubt the identity that the Father spoke over Him. This is what we will see the serpent do to Eve and Adam in the Garden.

Did you know Satan has only a few tricks, but they're on "repeat"? We will look at Jesus' victories closely later, but for now, just know that Jesus our Savior is prepared. He spent 40 days and 40 nights in fasting and prayer, possibly experiencing the most powerful revelation from the Holy Spirit and intimacy with the Father on earth that He would ever experience.

We will discuss this later, but Satan is attempting the same old tricks on Jesus that worked on Adam and Eve – doubt, pride and self-sufficiency. If you are "x", then you should be able to do "y".

Haven't we all fallen for this at some point? There are many people today, some even followers of Christ, who are stuck in this trap. We will delve into this more, but the deception is that you never arrive. The goalposts are always moving.

Jesus spoke these words: "For what does it profit a man to gain the whole world and to lose his soul?" (Mark 8:36, BLB). So, you see, the value of a person's soul can only be realized in God alone.

When a person has not found his true worth and value in God, he or she learns to cope with insecurities by projecting the image that we want others to see. We may be said to "wear a mask", to hide our inner struggle so others don't see our insecurities and pain. Many times, we don't even know that we are doing this because it has become a part of our personality and default behavior. Have you ever heard someone say, or even said yourself, "Well, that's just the way I am"? It's a justification not to change. We must allow ourselves to be transformed (Romans 12:2).

These insecurities manifest themselves in many ways, and if left unchecked, we can hurt even the ones we love. Some of the most common insecurities that plague us are fear, guilt, shame, worry, doubt, rejection, anger and depression.

Maybe you had a harsh or critical parent, so you became a "straight-A student" and you're striving to be accepted. Maybe you became the "ladies' man" or "the pretty girl", hiding behind looks for attention and validation.

Please, don't take on shame and guilt because you may experience some or many of these emotions. We are going to take a journey from Genesis to Revelation to reveal the most diabolical conspiracy against mankind - I call it, "The Fig Leaf Conspiracy."

We will discover why the fallen angel, cleverly disguised as a serpent, was intent on stripping man of the Glory covering of God and how God's plan for Recovery provided us with what we so desperately desire and long for... value and worth.

We will unpack the Genesis story to be reminded that the first man and woman, Adam and Eve, were made in the image and likeness of GOD (Genesis 1:26). They were the capstone and consummation of all creation.

At the end of the first five days of creation God proclaimed, "It is good". On the sixth day of creation, he made man and exclaimed, "It is very good!" (Genesis 1:31). The man and woman were described as "naked and unashamed" (Genesis 2:25). There was no shame because they were covered in the glory of God. They had no knowledge of shame or "nakedness". Through their disobedience, they forfeited this glorious covering and now needed to hide from God and "covered themselves with fig leaves". Hence, the Fig Leaf Conspiracy had begun.

Have you been hiding behind "fig leaves"? In the following chapters, we will look at some of the men and women of the Bible and discover God's Recovery Plan for them and for us all. Together, we will retire the fig leaves, embrace our Savior, and be restored in Christ's glory.

"To them God has chosen to make known among the Gentiles the glorious riches of this mystery, which is Christ in you, the hope of glory."
Colossians 1:27 (NIV)

Chapter 1

The Glory Covering

"Then God said, 'Let Us make man in Our image, according to Our likeness; let them have dominion over the fish of the sea, over the birds of the air, and over the cattle, over all the earth and over every creeping thing that creeps on the earth.' So God created man in His own image; in the image of God He created him; male and female He created them."
Genesis 1:26-27 (NKJV)

How does a gray rock provide light? The Greek philosopher Anaxagoras narrowly escaped execution 2,500 years ago for answering this question. He promoted the idea that the sun was a burning rock reflecting its light onto the moon, which he claimed was just a rock. By using simple geometry between the sun, moon and earth, he created models that predicted the moon's phases and eclipses (Warmflash, 2019).

He was thanked by being exiled, but today, we know he was correct - the moon has no light by itself. The light we see from the moon is really from the source, the sun. Did I mention how grateful I am to live in this day and age?

You were created to reflect God's light. Many people that I know, even some who have been believers in Christ for a long time, respond to such a statement with blushing and self-deprecation. I have actually had people tell me that they are nothing special and have no talents or abilities. When you take the focus off what you can or cannot do, centering in on Jesus Christ by faith and what He can do – then you are perfectly positioned to reflect HIS light!

Let's have an important conversation before we take the focus off "me, myself and I". Do you have an accurate, Biblical view of yourself? Does the church have an accurate, Biblical view of herself?

When I ask this question in meetings, usually people go silent. Sometimes, I get answers that are self-abasing and sometimes I get the encouragers charging in to declare that what God creates is wonderful (and they're not wrong). But I want to take you back to meet Adam and Eve, the first man and woman, to the beginning of creation.

Genesis 1:26 – 27 reveals: "In the beginning, God made man in HIS image and likeness."

What does this even mean? The word "image" used in Genesis 1:26 above is a Hebrew word that comes from a root word meaning "to shade," or "a phantom" and means "illusion, resemblance; hence, a representative figure" (from Strong's Concordance, H6754). You were created in God's "shade" and under His covering, intended to resemble Him and be His representative figure on earth! God designed us so that when others look at us, they see Him reflected back – like the moon reflects the sun. This is only possible by faith in the Son of God, Jesus Christ.

"The Son radiates God's own glory and expresses the very character of God, and he sustains everything by the mighty power of his command. When he had cleansed us from our sins, he sat down in the place of honor at the right hand of the majestic God in heaven. This shows that the Son is far greater than the angels, just as the name God gave him is greater than their names."
Hebrews 1:3-4 (NLT)

Man and woman, Adam and Eve, reflected God's image just as the moon reflects the sun's light. Before they fell, they were created with a beautiful covering of the glory of God. They didn't try to live their best life or make lists of things they needed to do – although they had a job in keeping the garden, Adam and Eve existed in a perpetual state of rest before the fall.

There are people that I know who work really hard. From dusk until dawn, they exert all their effort, striving to be good enough in everything that they do.

Let me preface this by pointing out that excellence is a priority. The Bible encourages us to do everything as unto the Lord (Colossians 3:23), and to do everything with all our might (Ecclesiastes 9:10)! Christians should never be mediocre. To the contrary, our employers and business partners should be astonished as we go above and beyond in whatever it is we are given to do. Excellence is a priority and becomes natural as we walk in the Spirit.

Have you ever met someone who is striving too hard? I know people that are "white-knuckling" their salvation journey – they have a morning routine list and an evening routine list full of religious activities. They have all the "Christianese" sayings down. They go to all the Christian events and say all the right Christian things, and they're always serving more than they should, but they don't get a bit of peace or rest.

Maybe this is even you. There is nothing wrong with being busy and productive, but part of the restoration that Jesus gave us involves setting aside striving that is based in works.

Hebrews 4:8 -11 declares, *"For if Joshua had given them rest, God would not have spoken later about another day. There remains, then, a Sabbath-rest for the people of God; for anyone who enters God's rest also rests from their works, just as God did from his. Let us, therefore, make every effort to enter that rest, so that no one will perish by following their example of disobedience."*

Adam and Eve (before they fell) were at complete rest and peace. Scripture reveals God's clear intent to restore us, not just to the original place of rest enjoyed briefly by Adam and Eve, but to an even higher place of rest – a spacious place obtained for us by Jesus Christ, paid for by His perfect blood.

"But God, who is rich in mercy, because of His great love with which He loved us, even when we were dead in trespasses, made us alive together with Christ (by grace you have been saved), and raised us up together, and made us sit together in the heavenly places in Christ Jesus, that in the ages to come He might show the exceeding riches of His grace in His kindness toward us in Christ Jesus."
Ephesians 2:4-7 (NKJV)

God created Adam and Eve with a brilliant covering of His glory, but He created them distinctly different - one man and one woman. We can speculate that Adam and Eve had little, if any, self-awareness of their beautiful covering of God's glory, except to the extent they admired it on each other. Have you ever noticed something amazing about another person, and they were not even fully aware until it was pointed out to them? Adam and Eve were free to be authentic without a second thought as they lived in His rest and peace.

Adam and Eve were naked, yet they were clothed, because they were covered with the thick, radiating light of God's glorious presence. They reflected God, who is light, and they were awesome to behold.

"This is the message which we have heard from Him and declare to you, that God is light and in Him is no darkness at all."
1 John 1:5 (NKJV)

Further in Genesis 2:25, we see that Adam and Eve are described as "naked and unashamed". They had an openness and transparency before God and each other without the presence of any fear whatsoever. This kind of openness and transparency came from rest and peace in the loving presence of the Lord.

"Those who look to him are radiant; their faces are never covered with shame."
Psalms 34:5 (NIV)

When my son was little, I educated him on the dangers of smoking cigarettes, as any parent does. One day when he was about five, we saw a neighbor standing outside her door with a lit cigarette in her hand. Before I could react, my son ran to her side, shouting: "Cigarettes will make you die!" Instead of becoming angry, she was so touched by his earnest, genuine concern that she put her cigarette out and sadly said, "I know, honey...I'm trying to stop."

If we dared to be who we are in Christ, the world would be turned upside-down. God is calling us into a higher level of glory – His radiant glory – that can only be found when we are free enough in Him to be transparent and authentic with the people around us. What if we were?

"When I consider Your heavens, the work of Your fingers, the moon and the stars, which You have ordained, What is man that You are mindful of him, And the son of man that You visit him? For You have made him a little lower than the angels, And You have crowned him with glory and honor.
You have made him to have dominion over the works of Your hands; You have put all things under his feet, All sheep and oxen— Even the beasts of the field, The birds of the air, And the fish of the sea That pass through the paths of the seas."
Psalm 8:3 – 8 (NKJV)

In the scriptures above, we find that man (Adam and Eve), and the Son of Man (Jesus) were "crowned with glory and honor." Let's break that down. In the Hebrew, the word for crown is "atar", which is interpreted as "to encircle or surround". Think about that! Man and woman are covered, encircled and surrounded by glory and honor.

When I use words like "glory" and "honor" with Generation Z (generally those born between late 1990s and early 2010s) and even Generation X (generally those born between 1965 and 1980), sometimes I get a blank stare in return because our culture doesn't use those words much anymore.

2,000 years of stained glass, dusty pews and hymnals cannot obscure the power of God's Word and His Spirit. Listen, I adore stained glass, pews and hymnals as much as any redeemed person, but let's bring manna to the thousands of young and middle-aged people who are hungering after something only God can give them.

In Matthew 13:52, Jesus instructs us: *"He said to them, 'Therefore every teacher of the law who has become a disciple in the kingdom of heaven is like the owner of a house who brings out of his storeroom new treasures as well as old.'"*

The words in the Bible are spirit and life. As Jesus tells us in John 6:63b (NKJV), "…The words that I speak to you are spirit, and they are life." He isn't just talking about the red letters in your Bible. Jesus IS the Word made flesh.

John 1:14 (NKJV) says, "And the Word became flesh and dwelt among us, and we beheld His glory, the glory as of the only begotten of the Father, full of grace and truth." As we take in God's Word, we are taking in His Spirit and life!

Going back to our question from Psalm 8:3 – 8 above - what do the words translated as "glory" and "honor" mean?

The two words that are interpreted here are "chabod" and "shekinah". "Chabod" is a Hebrew word that speaks of the weight of a copious amount of splendor (from Strong's H3519) and "shekinah" is defined as a brilliant light. This glory covering is what Adam and Eve wore at creation. Can you imagine? They were physically naked but spiritually covered, or clothed.

This caused them to be completely secure, open and transparent. They had no fear, anxiety, guilt, shame, rejection or any other negative feelings. When God came to walk with them in "the cool of the day" (Genesis 3:8), can you picture them drawing near to Him with complete transparency? They were perfect and sinless, in His image and likeness.

God is good (as we see throughout scripture, especially in Psalm 73:1 and I Timothy 4:4) and Adam and Eve knew goodness because they knew Him. They knew no evil or sin experientially before the fall.

However, God gave Adam and Eve a free will to choose. Otherwise, they would have been like robots. I believe in our day and time, that is termed "AI" (Artificial intelligence).

Imagine for a moment that Adam and Eve were created without free will – no personal agency, no ability to choose anything other than what God says. In that scenario, Adam and Eve would do as God asks every time because they are simply unable to do anything else. Doesn't that sound a little Orwellian to you? How is that any different from playing Minecraft? (Not that I know how!) God loves us, but He will not force His way. He wants you to choose Him.

It is also important at this time to point out that the word "covering" is closely related to the word "anointing." We will see how important this is as we move into subsequent chapters. Anointing means "to pour over, covering". The Spirit of God is the "anointing" and the Spirit of Glory (Isaiah 61:1, Luke 4:18, Acts 10:38, and 1 Peter 4:14).

God, in His infinite wisdom and goodness, will restore to us the lost "glory covering" with something greater than the original - but first, we're going to be spectators. Adam and Eve are going to forfeit their magnificent glory covering. We will expose the source of the conspiracy behind it and survey the tragic results that followed as we move on to "The Uncovering" in Chapter 2.

The Uncovering

*"And God blessed them, and God said unto them, Be
fruitful, and multiply, and replenish the earth, and subdue
it: and have dominion over the fish of the sea, and over
the fowl of the air, and over every living thing that
moveth upon the earth."*
Genesis 1:28-29, KJV

At creation, Adam and Eve were covered with God's glory
in perfection. Their covering exceeded Lucifer's as they
were made in the awesome image and likeness of God
(Genesis 1:26). This is where the Fig Leaf Conspiracy
unfolds.

Lucifer's jealousy of Adam and Eve – their relationship
with God, their incredible constitution, and their glorious
covering of God's light - is what led him to plot against
Adam and Eve in the Garden. As if that weren't enough,
Adam and Eve are appointed to multiply, take over and
rule over all of God's creation. They are commissioned to
"be fruitful, multiply, fill the Earth and subdue it".

We can miss the magnitude of this mandate if we skip
past it too quickly. When you consider what God gave
Adam and Eve, it's no surprise that an enemy came
slithering around, eager to lead Adam and Eve astray, to
lose their relationship with God, and then to steal their
position. (Where did he come from, anyway? We'll talk
about that soon).

In the last chapter, we demonstrated that you were created to reflect God's light. God's radiant glory presence surrounding Adam and Eve was part of who they were, but the creation mandate is what they were called to do. Have you noticed that many people seem lost with no purpose? We need to receive the creation mandate. When God tells Adam and Eve to "be fruitful, multiply, replenish the Earth and subdue it", what did He mean?

A concise breakdown of the original Hebrew reveals a few nuances. The first phrase, translated "be fruitful," is from the Hebrew word "para", which means "to bring forth, grow and increase" (Strong's H6509). That's pretty straightforward.

But the next word, translated "multiply", is a little more complex with more flavor. The word used here is "rabah", meaning: "to increase in whatever respect; bring in abundance; be in authority; continue, enlarge, excel, make great; to be more in number, give more in number and have more in number; to ask much, be much, gather much, take much and yield much; to multiply, nourish and be plenteous in the process of time" (Strong's H7235).

Don't miss God's heart here! "To increase in whatever respect...to be more, give more and have more...to be in authority?" What does that sound like to you? That sounds like God's plan for the believer – to increase in every area from glory to glory and faith to faith.

The third word of our creation mandate, translated "replenish", is the Hebrew word "mala", meaning "to accomplish, fulfill, consecrate, overflow, furnish, replenish, gather together, satisfy, have wholly." (Strong's H4390). In summary, the first three words speak of growth, radical increase through time overflowing to those around you, and completion, with only a subtle connotation to "having authority."

But the last word here is different - the Hebrew verb "kabas" that we translate as "subdue", means "to tread down, conquer, bring into subjection" (Strong's H3533). Like a fortissimo after a crescendo, this word speaks of man and woman "having all things under their feet."

Put the Hebrew words together, and what do you notice? "Para, rabah, mala et eres, kabas..." They rhyme! God's rhythm here would have been catchy and easy to remember to a Hebrew. In English, it might be as if He said, "Sow, grow, overflow, and then overthrow." We're wired to fulfill the creation mandate.

One precious family we know had a son named Bobby who beat childhood cancer twice before passing away of a third cancer at age 20. When he was about 13 or 14, while his cancer was in remission, he was attending public school.

One day, while running track and field, a classmate dropped dead right in front of him. From that point on, Bobby became passionate about sharing Jesus with his friends, having great impact.

At age 20, the third cancer returned and he had months to live. When Bobby confided to his dad that he felt he didn't do anything for God, His dad reminded him of all the people he influenced, pointing out that if even one person got saved from his witness, and then that person shares Christ with others, then yes, he had done something for God. For Bobby, this settled the matter. The question in his heart was, "Did I fulfill the mandate?"

Psalm 8:6-8 (NKJV) declares: "You have made him to have dominion over the works of Your hands; You have put all things under his feet, All sheep and oxen— Even the beasts of the field, The birds of the air, And the fish of the sea That pass through the paths of the seas."

Adam and Eve were given authority over every living thing on Earth. In essence, God made them vice-lords of creation and we see that in Psalm 8:6-8 above. He set them in the midst of the Garden of Eden and said they could eat of any tree except the Tree of the Knowledge of Good and Evil. Their options included the Tree of Life. Remember, the Holy Spirit is the ONE who gives life (John 6:63) which includes eternal life. Which tree do you think God was hoping they would choose?

Now, let's focus on the Tree of Knowledge of Good and Evil. If Adam and Eve ate from the tree that produced that fruit, they would die. Notice that all the trees were pleasant to the sight and good for food (Gen 2:9), not just the forbidden tree. Again, they were created with free will to choose.

"Now the serpent was more cunning than any beast of the field which the Lord God had made. And he said to the woman, "Has God indeed said, 'You shall not eat of every tree of the garden'?" And the woman said to the serpent, "We may eat the fruit of the trees of the garden; but of the fruit of the tree which is in the midst of the garden, God has said, 'You shall not eat it, nor shall you touch it, lest you die.' Then the serpent said to the woman, "You will not surely die. For God knows that in the day you eat of it your eyes will be opened, and you will be like God, knowing good and evil."
Genesis 3:1-4 (NKJV)

Enter here the serpent, who is identified by various names throughout Scripture, such as the Devil, Satan and Beelzebub. He is also known as Lucifer, shining one, and son of the dawn (Isaiah 14:12).

He existed before the Genesis narrative. He was a beautiful guardian and covering cherub (Ezekiel 28:16) or angel. We get insight into who he was and what he did when we study God's judgments against the kings of Babylon and Tyre in Isaiah 14 and Ezekiel 28. Both kings were filled with pride and proclamations of self-deification. The prophecies reveal who was behind their arrogant ways and presumptuous attitudes (Ezekiel 28:5, 17; Isaiah 14:13-14).

Before the fall, Lucifer was described as the seal of perfection, full of wisdom, perfect in beauty. He was in Eden, the Garden of God. He had a covering of his own – a golden chestplate covered in precious stones (Ezekiel 28:12,13,17), which he lost when God kicked him out of heaven.

Like I mentioned earlier, Adam and Eve's covering exceeded Lucifer's as they were made in the image and likeness of God. (Gen 1:26). Let's keep in mind here what Scripture reveals in James 4:16: "where jealousy, envy and selfishness exist, there is disorder and every evil practice."

A conspiracy speaks of a plot or collusion. Satan envied Adam and Eve's relationship with God, their amazing frames and the glory that surrounded them like a covering, which he had lost. This intense jealousy and hatred is what led him, working through the serpent, to plot against Adam and Eve.

"Then war broke out in heaven. Michael and his angels fought against the dragon, and the dragon and his angels fought back. But he was not strong enough, and they lost their place in heaven. The great dragon was hurled down—that ancient serpent called the devil, or Satan, who leads the whole world astray. He was hurled to the earth, and his angels with him."
Revelation 12:7-9 (NIV)

When Lucifer became filled with pride and sought to excel and ascend higher than the most high God, war broke out in heaven, ending with Satan and one-third of the angels who sided with him being hurled down to earth.

Don't miss how Satan was described: "...that ancient serpent called the devil, or Satan, who leads the whole world astray." What was Satan trying to do in Genesis 1:28? Consistent with his fallen description, he was leading Eve and Adam astray. Although the Bible doesn't explicitly state the timing of Lucifer's fall, we can probably hang our hat here, based on these and other scriptures. It is our position that Satan was fallen when he succeeded in leading Adam and Eve astray into sin, bringing death into the entire world.

Lucifer's pride is especially revealed in Isaiah 14:

"How you are fallen from heaven, O Lucifer, son of the morning! How you are cut down to the ground, You who weakened the nations! For you have said in your heart: 'I will ascend into heaven, I will exalt my throne above the stars of God; I will also sit on the mount of the congregation On the farthest sides of the north; I will ascend above the heights of the clouds, I will be like the Most High.' Yet you shall be brought down to Sheol, To the lowest depths of the Pit."
Isaiah 14:12-15 (NKJV)

Look at Lucifer's thoughts just before he was thrown from heaven:

1. "I will" ascend to the heavens above God.

2. "I will" set my throne.

3. "I will" rule on the Mountain of the assembly.

4. "I will" climb to the top of the clouds.

5. "I will" make myself like the MOST HIGH.

Focus on the "I wills". This is the crux of how Satan tempts Eve to eat the forbidden fruit.

There are glaring self-assertions that we need to take note of in our lives. I call those, the "I, me and my", which speak to self (selfish, self-centeredness, and self-absorption).

Lucifer lost his anointed covering of precious stones as a guardian angel because of pride. He was brought down very low and was thrown out of heaven forever. Many theologians believe that is when his name was changed to Satan.

Isaiah 14 and Ezekiel 28 start off declaring God's judgments upon King Babylon and King Tyre for their evil acts, and then segues into declarations of judgment upon Satan himself (Is 14:15; Ez 28:17). These two chapters show us who was behind the judgments of these two earthly kings. We can see that Satan uses demonic influence to deceive people, sometimes even well-meaning people, into acting on his promptings because of selfishness. This gives us insight into Jesus' response to Peter when this disciple rebuked Him for saying He was going to die. Jesus said, "Get behind me Satan (adversary), you have the things of man in mind and not the things of God" (Mark 8:33). He was not calling Peter "Satan". He was identifying what and who was behind his rebuke. The same holds true with the Kings of Babylon and Tyre and the serpent in the garden.

"When the woman saw that the fruit of the tree was good for food and pleasing to the eye, and also desirable for gaining wisdom, she took some and ate it. She also gave some to her husband, who was with her, and he ate it. Then the eyes of both of them were opened, and they realized they were naked; so they sewed fig leaves together and made coverings for themselves."
Genesis 3:6-7 (NIV)

Now, Serpent's approach to Eve is established in Genesis 3, where he is described as shrewd and subtle. He asked her, "Has God said, 'you shall not eat of every tree in the garden'?" Eve answered that they could not eat from the tree in the midst of the garden or touch it lest they die. She acknowledged that they could eat from all the other trees except the Tree of Knowledge of Good and Evil. Then the serpent, Satan in disguise, said, "You surely will not die, for God knows in the day you eat of it, you will be like Him" (Genesis 3:5). Satan is subtly presenting pride and self-reliance to Eve when he says, "You will" be like God.

This boils down to one question- will she choose "my will" or "Thy will, God?" Will she choose "me" over "Thee"? What will we choose?

A friend of our ministry shared about a time he found a wallet on the ground. He was leaving a convenience store, and there was a fat wallet on the ground full of money. There was no one around to see what he would do, and he could really use the money inside. He took the wallet inside, spoke with the convenience store clerk, and they looked up the owner's phone number and called him to notify him that he left his wallet at the convenience store.

It turns out that the large amount of money stuffed in the man's wallet was rent money. Needless to say, the owner showed up quickly, so distraught about losing the wallet, he didn't thank anyone – just left in a hurry.

Not long after that, my friend left his own wallet sitting on top of a payphone and drove away. He was in the next city before he realized his wallet was missing, and then had to drive all the way back. Hours later, in the dark of night, he got back to that payphone - lo and behold, his wallet, still containing all his money, was sitting right where he left it.

We don't give the enemy any unnecessary attention, but we are not to be ignorant of Satan's devices (2 Corinthians 2:11b). Satan comes to steal, kill and destroy (John 10:10a) and to lead the world astray.

As the Lord described him in James 3:16 (NKJV): "Wherever envy and self-seeking exist, confusion and every evil thing are there."

Satan's goal was to strip Adam and Eve of their anointed covering and steal their position of authority. The serpent's shrewd words sowed doubt in Eve to cause her to question whether God was keeping something good from her.

As Adam and Eve take the fruit and eat, evil and death overtake them, although it is not immediate. Adam and Eve, beloved by God, carrying a powerful mandate, are now fallen and covered with reproach, naked and experiencing shame.

What do they do next? Genesis 3:7 says "their eyes were opened, and they knew they were naked and sewed together fig leaves" to cover themselves. In this way, the Fig Leaf Conspiracy was born.

Chapter 3

The Great Cover Up

"Then the eyes of both of them were opened, and they knew that they were naked; and they sewed fig leaves together and made themselves coverings. And they heard the sound of the Lord God walking in the garden in the cool of the day, and Adam and his wife hid themselves from the presence of the Lord God among the trees of the garden. Then the Lord God called to Adam and said to him, "Where are you?" So he said, "I heard Your voice in the garden, and I was afraid because I was naked; and I hid myself."
Genesis 3:7-10 (NKJV)

Have you ever had something go totally wrong and your actions next make even less sense? Adam and Eve's eyes are opened, but they are not like God – they just realize with horror that they are naked, so they begin the arduous process of covering themselves by sewing together fig leaves.

Can you imagine how long this took? Where did they even get a needle and thread? It isn't like Adam and Eve were experienced clothing manufacturers or had any idea how to make the hems line up.

Have you ever tried to actually sew leaves together? They are irregularly shaped and tear easily. I'm sure every time Adam sat down, he needed a repair. Needless to say, I don't think that DIY project came out too well.

But this isn't just a failed crafting project – Adam and Eve, God's glorious creation, are naked and fallen, covering themselves and hiding. Upon eating of the tree of forbidden fruit, they lost their covering of God's glory. Desperate to cover their shame, Adam and Eve select fig leaves as material, but their efforts only produce badly-fitting "clothing" prone to tear and cause further embarrassment. Worst of all, God is the last one they want to see. Their world is completely upside down.

Idolatry is the worship of anything other than God. The scriptures below from Romans reveal that fallen man, in his own "wisdom," exchanges the glory of God for idolatry. In other scriptures in the Bible, idolatry is sometimes interchangeable with self-deification (see Colossians 3:5).

"Claiming to be wise, they instead became utter fools.
And instead of worshiping the glorious, ever-living God,
they worshiped idols made to look like mere people and
birds and animals and reptiles."
Romans 1:22-23 (NIV)

Our view is distorted when Jesus is not first. Without Him, we become degraded, replacing foolish things with what is wise. Adam and Eve are a great example - they traded the glory of God for fig leaves because of the suggestion they would be "like God" if they went against Him.

What we saw with Lucifer in the Bible (Isaiah chapter 14 and Ezekiel chapter 28), we can see now with Adam and Eve - "I will be like God." Recall Lucifer's thoughts just before he was thrown from heaven (Isaiah 14:12-15, NKJV):

1. "I will" ascend to the heavens above God.

2. "I will" set my throne.

3. "I will" rule on the Mountain of the assembly.

4. "I will" climb to the top of the clouds.

5. "I will" make myself like the MOST HIGH.

As Adam and Eve sewed together these fig leaves, maybe they were pleased to have a solution to the problem of the nakedness. Maybe, for a moment, Adam and Eve felt relieved by their new invention of clothing, or even a little bit proud of their problem-solving abilities in this new, terrible place of self-reliance.

Have you ever known someone that always had to "keep up with the Joneses"? For example, a dear friend shared with me that they had their pool resurfaced and remodeled, it being about 20 years overdue, and for fun, added a small waterfall. Not long after that, despite a perfectly good pool - their neighbor got theirs done too, with a paved driveway to boot.

Earlier, we mentioned the putting on of masks, putting up fronts and projecting images. Shame has a whole cast of characters: fear, guilt, anxiety, rejection, to name a few.

We have an inner drive to display that we are "good enough." Sometimes external things are how people choose to demonstrate they are worthy. Adam and Eve sewed together fig leaves – fallen people today buy large houses, wear designer clothes, accumulate trophies, get plastic surgery, and obtain degrees and credentials.

Many times, these trappings are modern-day fig leaves - a self-made covering to hide those emotions, feelings and issues that one struggles with.

That is what naked, fallen man does. He refuses to deal with issues, and eventually this can lead to mental, emotional, or even physical problems.

"Cover-ups" promote a person's value by what they wear, possess, or even who they have relationships with - whatever will display or validate their worth, but they are a trap. Eventually, they tear and cause embarrassment.

After nearly 30 years of being the dean of admissions at the prestigious university Massachusetts Institute of Technology, Marilee Jones made a shocking public confession: she fabricated the academic credentials on her resume and was resigning from her revered position.

Previously, she was a leading public figure in the field of college admissions and a successful author, but the spectacle ruined her reputation almost immediately. One anonymous tip to administration ten days prior prompted an internal inquiry, destroying a 28-year public persona in the making. (Lewin, 2007)

Listen, the Bible is my authority. We don't give credence to the latest trends in worldly, human philosophies (Colossians 2:8), but there is an interesting observation in the field of psychology for us to consider.

When people take actions that contradict their deepest held beliefs, it creates a stressful mental state called, "cognitive dissonance". This theory holds that people desire consistency in their beliefs and actions, and in response to the stress of cognitive dissonance, they will either change their actions or change their beliefs to alleviate the discomfort (Saul McLeod, 2023). The bigger the difference between our actions and our held beliefs, the greater the pressure experienced. Cognitive dissonance generates anxiety and guilt, and left unresolved, is associated with depression and mental illness.

In fact, one study in particular found that people who suffered from depression reported experiencing prolonged periods of cognitive dissonance in higher levels, and made less efforts to reduce dissonance than non-depressed participants in the study (Mark Byrne, Agnes Higgins, & Jan de Vries, 2023). None of the authors here are psychologists, and depression has many factors, but the findings are clear – people desire for their deepest held beliefs and outward actions to match.

So why fig leaves? After a tragic fall, we know Adam and Eve were ashamed and had a compulsion to hide and cover up. But fig leaves? I propose to you that there was a strategic reason for their choice – not Adam and Eve's strategy, because they are definitely winging it – but God's strategy. Let's talk about the significance of figs.

Could the tree of the knowledge of good and evil have been a fig tree? Let's examine the vehicle that brought the curse and death when Adam and Eve lost their covering. When we consider the prophetic and implied meanings given to the fig tree and the fig itself in scripture, we begin to see certain parallels between the fig tree and the tree of knowledge of good and evil. There are several sections of Scripture that refer to this tree and its fruit, and the fall and cover up that followed.

First, fig trees are large, growing as high as 30 feet. Second, the figs would have been readily available, pleasant to the eye and good for food.

In the Bible, figs represent peace, prosperity, judgment and Israel itself (Hosea 9:10 and Jeremiah 24:1-10). Adam and Eve had complete peace and prosperity in the Garden of Eden until they ate from the tree of the knowledge of good and evil, releasing sin, death and judgment into the whole world.

Old covenant law would be needed next - to reveal sin and point us to the coming Messiah. The fig is a complete picture of the fall.

"When I found Israel, it was like finding grapes in the desert; when I saw your ancestors, it was like seeing the early fruit on the fig tree."
Hosea 9:10 (NIV)

The one tree that Adam and Eve were forbidden to eat the fruit from represented their free will to choose, echoing Deuteronomy 30:19b (NKJV), "… I have set before you life and death, blessing and cursing; therefore choose life, that both you and your descendants may live."

Knowing that figs represent judgment and Israel (Jeremiah 24:1-10), it follows that the tree to bring either prosperity or judgment on Adam and Eve could be a fig tree. Old Testament law (the first 5 books of the Bible) points us to the Messiah, but what pointed us to the law? Sin's entrance into the world through Adam and Eve eating a fig.

"But the Law came to increase and expand [the awareness of] the trespass [by defining and unmasking sin]."
Romans 5:20(a), AMP

Law became necessary once sin entered the world at the fall. Through Moses, God laid out a standard of good and evil designed to reveal sin. What was the tree in the garden named again? "The Tree of the Knowledge of Good and Evil." How do we measure something as good or evil? By the law. Restraining from eating the fig brought peace and prosperity, but once eaten, it ushered in judgment and law.

"Nevertheless, I would not have known what sin was had it not been for the law. For I would not have known what coveting really was if the law had not said, 'You shall not covet.' But sin, seizing the opportunity afforded by the commandment, produced in me every kind of coveting."
Romans 7:7b-8a (NIV)

Think of the Law for a moment. Through Old Testament law, God reveals that man cannot make himself right. These words are repeated throughout the Law: "Thou shall...," and "Thou shall not...". It represents a choice, and the Law beckons man to choose life.

"I have set before you life and death; blessing and cursing; therefore, choose life." (Deuteronomy 30:18) The law is holy, yet man is totally unable to follow it.

"Once I was alive apart from the law; but when the commandment came, sin sprang to life and I died. I found that the very commandment that was intended to bring life actually brought death. For sin, seizing the opportunity afforded by the commandment, deceived me, and through the commandment put me to death."
Romans 7:9-11 (NIV)

What did God promise would happen if Adam and Eve ate from the fruit of the tree of knowledge of good and evil? He promised: *"... for in the day that you eat of it you shall surely die."* Romans 8:2 calls the law, "the law of sin and death".

Eating of the tree of knowledge of good and evil brought death and a choice. The Law was given to reveal that man's willpower cannot please God and justify man. When Jesus came to the earth, the only ones we ever saw Him angry with were the moneychangers and the self-righteous.

"For they being ignorant of God's righteousness, and seeking to establish their own righteousness, have not submitted to the righteousness of God."
Romans 10:3 (NKJV)

Jesus was angry with the Pharisees because they tried to establish their own righteousness apart from God. This is the same old idea from the Garden of Eden - "I will be like God."

I submit that the selfish nature – I like to call it the "I, me, and my" - is the flesh that is at enmity with God (Romans 8:7), and it does not submit to the Law of God, nor is it able to do so. A quick skim of Romans tells us that sin lives in our flesh, and no one is able to follow the whole Law.

"What shall we conclude then? Do we have any advantage? Not at all! For we have already made the charge that Jews and Gentiles alike are all under the power of sin. As it is written: 'There is no one righteous, not even one; there is no one who understands; there is no one who seeks God. All have turned away, they have together become worthless; there is no one who does good, not even one.'"

Romans 3:9-12 (NIV)

God never intended mankind to be under the Law permanently. The Law is likened to a tutor or a teacher that gives us the knowledge of our sin (Galatians 3:24; Romans 3:20,28; Galatians 2:16). It cannot be kept by man's force of will because it focuses on the man and his efforts; however, God who is the great I AM says, "I will - if you believe in my Son".

"Therefore the law was our tutor to bring us to Christ, that we might be justified by faith."
Galatians 3:24 (NKJV)

For these reasons, we consider the fig tree as the tree that brought death, a curse, and later, the law and Israel – embodying the prophetic picture of the fig.

"Jesus saw Nathanael coming toward Him, and said of him, 'Behold, an Israelite indeed, in whom is no deceit!' Nathanael said to Him, 'How do You know me?' Jesus answered and said to him, 'Before Philip called you, when you were under the fig tree, I saw you.' Nathanael answered and said to Him, 'Rabbi, You are the Son of God! You are the King of Israel!' Jesus answered and said to him, "Because I said to you, 'I saw you under the fig tree,' do you believe? You will see greater things than these.""
John 1:47-50 (NKJV)

As Phillip was bringing Nathaniel to meet Jesus, declaring they found the Messiah, Nathaniel's response was less than enthusiastic: "Can anything good come out of Nazareth?"

Yet, as they approached, Jesus exclaims, "Behold, a true Israelite without guile!" A Jewish belief was that the place of meditating on the Law was under the fig tree. Jesus knew that Nathaniel was meditating on Psalm 34:12-13: "What man is he that desireth life, and loveth many days, that he may see good? Keep thy tongue from evil, and thy lips from speaking guile." Nathanael's meditation under the fig tree was to be a man without guile. When Jesus calls this out to Nathaniel, it shook Nathaniel to his core, causing him to cry out, "You are the Messiah!"

When Jesus cursed the fig tree on the Mount of Olives a few days before His crucifixion, it wasn't the season for figs. Was He purposely cursing the vehicle that brought sin, judgment, death and law?

Jesus took death and the curse upon Himself when He was crucified on a tree. Is it possible that our Lord Jesus may have been crucified on the wood of a fig tree? As high as 30 feet... it is within the realm of possibility. Galatians 3:13 (NKJV) declares, "Christ has redeemed us from the curse of the Law, having become a curse for us, for it is written, "Cursed is everyone who hangs on a tree".

Satan comes after your glory-covering, the God-given identity that only you can walk out, so that you will waste your time covering yourself with dead works that don't fit you anyway.

> *"They looked to Him and were radiant, And their faces were not ashamed."*
> Psalm 34:5 (NKJV)

If you know Jesus Christ, you are redeemed from the curse and free in Him! He wishes to anoint us with the radiance of His countenance. You are called to shine with the glory of God!

Therefore, let us take off any cover ups, masks, and projected fronts. Who did He really create you to be? Let us desire His glory presence so we can reflect His light and fulfill our mandate.

Come on, God didn't create you to sit and soak in great messages at church. He made you to BE a great message! Even as Jesus prayed, "...glorify your son that your son might glorify you" (John 17:1), we pray that you will reflect His glory to win those in darkness. There are people looking for a way out!

After their conversation in the Garden of Eden about what has happened, God comes to Adam and Eve to supply a measure of recovery. His temporary solution for them, which is new clothes made from animal skins, lays the foundation for us to experience a full recovery and return to God's original intention.

Chapter 4

Discovery

"And they heard the sound of the Lord God walking in the garden in the cool of the day, and Adam and his wife hid themselves from the presence of the Lord God among the trees of the garden. Then the Lord God called to Adam and said to him, "Where are you?"
Genesis 3:8-9 (NKJV)

The plane went into a nosedive, slamming passengers and flight crew into the ceiling and overhead bins of the packed Air Canada flight, travelers screaming in terror. Coming dangerously close to another plane, the pilot snapped out of his disoriented state just in time, pulling the plane back into the proper flight path.

After landing, investigators questioned the pilot about the incident. On that particular night, the planet Venus shone so brightly that the exhausted pilot mistook it for an oncoming plane – jamming the nose of aircraft towards the earth, injuring 16 passengers in the process. (ABC News, 2012)

When God came to Adam and Eve in the garden as usual, during the cool of the day, they are missing. God calls out to them, "Where are you"?

Of course, He knew where they were and why they were hiding. God, who knows the answers, still asks them because He wants us to come to the Truth. He is the Truth and desires truth in the inner man (Psalm 51:6). He came to reveal what they have concealed because He comes to heal and not to harm.

God is drawing Adam and Eve back into relationship with Him because that's what He desires. When we see Jesus, He comes to seek and save that which has been lost (Luke 19:5-10). Of course, this is what He says when He calls Zaccheus, the notorious chief of the tax collectors.

God's questions are to bring us to a place of agreement which involves confession. Then, we can walk together in a relationship. Our God is a Reconciler and Restorer. He comes to bring the process of recovery, but first we have to get to a place of agreement with Him. That's why Amos 3:3 says, "Can two walk together, unless they are agreed?" God calls to them, "Where are you?"

"'Come now, let us reason together, says the LORD: though your sins are like scarlet, they shall be as white as snow; though they are red like crimson, they shall become like wool.'"
Isaiah 1:18 (ESV)

Jesus Christ is the same yesterday, today and forever – no matter what you have done or how far you have wandered off, He desires to draw you back to Himself. God's heart is to reconcile Adam and Eve back to Himself.

*"I drew them with gentle cords, with bands of love, And I
was to them as those who take the yoke from their neck.
I stooped and fed them."*
Hosea 11:4 (NKJV)

Let's think about the disoriented pilot for a moment. He
saw the planet Venus and thought it was an oncoming
plane. Losing all sense of direction, he points the airplane
into a nearly vertical trajectory, narrowly missing another
plane. The pilot no longer knew which way was up or
down, so he flew in the wrong direction with hundreds of
souls on board. This condition is called "spatial
disorientation", and it happens when pilots lose visual
references while flying. (Spatial Disorientation: Confusion
that Kills, n.d.)

Adam and Eve are experiencing the same type of deadly
confusion – they have sinned, lost their reference point for
direction (God), and now they're running, hiding and
wearing fig leaves for clothing.

A few years ago, a dear friend's teenage son began
working out with an award-winning personal trainer.
During the initial consultation, the trainer asked about his
goals. Initially, their son was light on details, but the
personal trainer pressed him, explaining, "I may know
what you are going to say, but I want to hear you say it."
After a year of consistency, time and efforts, their
determined son gained confidence, muscles and health.
It began with his own discovery and then "confession" of
what he wanted to change.

It's impressive when people accomplish goals after self-reflection, but supernatural miracles take place when you confess your sins to God in the name of Jesus.

"If we confess our sins, He is faithful and just to forgive us our sins and to cleanse us from all unrighteousness."
1 John 1:9 (NKJV)

God does two things when we confess our sins to Him – He forgives us, and He cleanses us from all unrighteousness. God's supernatural power is released when we confess our sins to Him.

Did you know that young people are coming to Christ in numbers we haven't seen in 50 years? Between 2019 and 2025, the numbers of Millennials (born between 1981 and 1996) and Generation Z (born between 1997 and 2012) claiming a commitment to Jesus Christ increased by 22-25%. When you drill into the statistics, Millennial men coming to Christ increased by 19 percent over the last six years, and Millennial women by six percent! When you look at Gen Z, the men coming to faith in Christ increased by 15 percent, and women by 7 percent from 2019 to 2025 (Barna.com, 2025). You've been hearing people say church is dying, but I've got news for you, friends – God is just getting started! He is drawing the youth to Himself, to arise and take their place in Him. Even now, God calls out to them…"Where are you?"

"He sent from above, He took me; He drew me out of many waters."
Psalm 18:16 (NKJV)

Remember, in their previous state of being covered by God's glory, Adam and Eve were wrapped in perfect LOVE, which is void of fear (John 4:18). At that time, Jesus had not yet come and died and rose again. There wasn't old covenant law yet either (which God is about to implement). After Adam and Eve fell, there was not yet any remittance for sins - only a fiery expectation of judgment.

"If we deliberately keep on sinning after we have received the knowledge of the truth, no sacrifice for sins is left, but only a fearful expectation of judgment and of raging fire that will consume the enemies of God."
Hebrews 10:26-27 (NIV)

God promised Adam and Eve that they would surely die in the day they eat of the fruit of the tree of knowledge of good and evil. So far they were just naked, but I'm sure they were waiting for death to show up at any moment. At this point, Adam and Eve are experiencing fear, shame, and a sense of foreboding.

But when God calls out to Adam, "Where are you?"... the sound of His voice re-orients them. Suddenly Adam and Eve remember which way is "up". Suddenly the ground isn't wobbling underneath them anymore, and their mind is clearing. His voice cuts through the confusion in their minds. "Where are you?" Adam knows that he must give an answer to Him who speaks.

"But the Lord God called to the man, "Where are you?" He answered, "I heard you in the garden, and I was afraid because I was naked; so I hid."
Genesis 3:9-10 (NIV)

Did he really just tell God, "You scared me because you called when I was naked?" God, could you please knock before you sneak up on us in the garden? Adam almost sounds like he's trying to be modest. But Adam wasn't afraid because he was NAKED – he was afraid because he ate the fruit God said not to eat.

Listen, God approves of manners and propriety, but it's reasonable to say here that Adam is giving a surface answer.

Have you ever asked someone an accountability question, and they give you a surface answer? The Pharisees in Jesus' day would master this technique of dodging accountability while maintaining an appearance of propriety – religiosity, the ultimate mask.

Adam's flimsy answer only gives him away, and God continues the process to help them discover their cover up.

"And he said, 'Who told you that you were naked? Have you eaten from the tree that I commanded you not to eat from?' The man said, 'The woman you put here with me—she gave me some fruit from the tree, and I ate it.' Then the Lord God said to the woman, 'What is this you have done?' The woman said, "The serpent deceived me, and I ate."'
Genesis 3:11-13 (NIV)

When God gets a little more direct, Adam resists the truth and shifts the blame on Eve. It is true that the Serpent first reasoned with Eve, but Adam was there and could have put a stop to the temptation.

Adam not only pointed to his wife but also shifts blame on God by saying, "it was the woman You gave me" (Genesis 3:12). In order to avoid taking responsibility, he pointed to Eve and God Himself. Then Eve followed suit by blaming the Serpent.

Blame shifting is so typical; rather than taking responsibility, we blame parents, siblings, peers and so on. Both avoided coming to the truth by resisting confession and reconciliation.

Her little brother was quiet and well-behaved, the kind of kid that flew under the radar most of the time and got good grades. After school, they went to a babysitter's house, a stout country woman, who watched about ten other school-age kids until their parents came to pick them up. One day after school, a rowdy boy named Jeffrey knocked over and broke a vase in the babysitter's house.

The babysitter lined all the kids up and demanded to know who broke the vase, cigarette hanging out of her lip, sweat beading on her forehead. Everyone was silent until Jeffrey exclaimed, "It was him!", pointing to her little brother.

The babysitter ushered all the kids out of the house and spanked the wrong kid with a flyswatter, and his anguished cries could be heard throughout the backyard. The boy's older sister ran as hard as she could, jumping on Jeffrey, pummeling the smaller boy with her fists, as the kids stood in a circle shouting, "Fight! Fight! Fight!"

You can come to God with gut-level honesty about who you've been and what you've done. If you confess with your mouth, Jesus is Lord, and believe that God raised Him from the dead, you will be saved (Romans 10:9). When you turn from your sin to agree with Him, He makes all things new (2 Corinthians 5:17).

He isn't going to kick you when you're down – He embraces, forgives and cleanses you of all unrighteousness. In Christ, you are not what you have done, and you are not what people have said about you. You have the power to become who God created you to be, but it begins when you get alone and get honest with God. Discovery leads to recovery.

"And Jacob was left alone, and a Man wrestled with him until daybreak. And when [the Man] saw that He did not prevail against [Jacob], He touched the hollow of his thigh; and Jacob's thigh was put out of joint as he wrestled with Him. Then He said, Let Me go, for day is breaking. But [Jacob] said, I will not let You go unless You declare a blessing upon me. [The Man] asked him, What is your name? And [in shock of realization, whispering] he said, Jacob [supplanter, schemer, trickster, swindler]! And He said, Your name shall be called no more Jacob [supplanter], but Israel [contender with God]; for you have contended and have power with God and with men and have prevailed."
Genesis 32:24-28 (AMPC)

This mysterious set of verses is a symbolic picture of salvation and personal transformation found in the Old Testament. You know, the part of the Bible that people largely dismiss?

Here we have a perfect picture of confession, repentance and restoration. When the "Man" (pre-incarnate Jesus) asked Jacob his name, Jacob realized (with horror) his true nature, acknowledging and confessing with sorrow that he was exactly what his name meant.

In response, God honors Jacob by changing his name and giving him a new, glorious identity. Jacob the Schemer became Israel the Victorious. God has the same thing for you!

Notice that God starts by asking Jacob: "What is your name?" God desires for each of us to become a new creation in Christ, but to get there, we need truth in the inward parts.

Ironically, the moment we acknowledge and confess, He forgives us and cleanses us from all unrighteousness. Why is it so hard to just get super blunt about our shortcomings with God? The moment we acknowledge, confess and turn to God from sin, God is there waiting for you - with your new, true identity. Discovery leads to restoration!

"And the Lord God made for Adam and for his wife garments of skins and clothed them."
Genesis 3:21 (ESV)

So how does a holy God have relationship with sinful man?

Atonement means to make amends for or to cover for sin. In Genesis 3:21, after specifically addressing their sins and issuing certain judgments, God brought clothing made from animal skins to Adam and Eve to cover them and obviously the fig leaves were removed. In Hebrews 9:22, the Scripture reads, "without the shedding of blood, there is no remission of sin."

Is it too much to suggest that God came to them with a lamb under His arm to atone for, (and cover) their sin? With this act of requiring a blood sacrifice for sin, the old covenant, or what will be Israel, is born.

"The Lord God made garments of skin for Adam and his wife and clothed them. And the Lord God said, "The man has now become like one of us, knowing good and evil. He must not be allowed to reach out his hand and take also from the tree of life and eat, and live forever." So the Lord God banished him from the Garden of Eden to work the ground from which he had been taken. After he drove the man out, he placed on the east side of the Garden of Eden cherubim and a flaming sword flashing back and forth to guard the way to the tree of life."
Genesis 3:21-24 (NIV)

The result of Adam and Eve's disobedience has severe consequences. They were prevented from re-entering the garden and eating from the tree of Life, which would have caused them to live forever and be eternally fallen like Satan's fallen angels – a consequence God was unwilling to risk.

Ultimate recovery would be made available to mankind through God sending His Son, Jesus Christ at the perfect time, to restore all that Adam and Eve abdicated when the Serpent beguiled them with his conspiracy to strip them of the Glory covering that they once wore. God has a plan for the redemption of all humanity, and He is going to implement it, piece by piece, like a Master Architect.

God is the master of relationships, and He knows the end from the beginning. He questions us to reveal our cover-up, atone for sin and bring restoration. Consider people such as Cain, Hagar, Jacob, the woman at the well, and others. "Cain, why are you angry? Where is your brother Abel?", "Hagar, where have you come from, where are you going"? "Jacob, what is your name"? Woman at the well, "Go, call your husband, and come back." The Lord even asks Satan in Job 1:7, "Where have you come from?"

These are questions we should honestly ask ourselves. His voice echoes through generations past, calling out to each of us: "Where are you?"

Chapter 5

The Unmasking

"I sought the Lord, and he answered me;
he delivered me from all my fears.
Those who look to him are radiant;
their faces are never covered with shame."
Psalm 34:4-5 (NIV)

She came gliding out of the dressing room onto the stage, her toes pressing into the front of her five-inch heels, and the audience drew forward to the edge. The men stood with money in their hands, raising it to get her attention. Nausea punched her in the stomach as the spotlight brightened, blinding her, and a voice like her father's gently declared: "They are worshiping you." She finished her set as quickly as she could, but that night, she went home different.

She drove to her tiny apartment, saying, "Jesus, Jesus, Jesus..." Suddenly, His name was the most beautiful name she had ever heard.

The next morning, she packed her bag with items from her former life and slung it into the dumpster with complete abandon. Her new life with Jesus had begun.

To Adam and Eve, God asks, "Where are you?" God's call rings out to the lost and fallen. But for everyone who comes to Him, He then asks: "What is your name?"

"[The Man] asked him, What is your name? And [in shock of realization, whispering] he said, Jacob [supplanter, schemer, trickster, swindler]! And He said, Your name shall be called no more Jacob [supplanter], but Israel [contender with God]; for you have contended and have power with God and with men and have prevailed."
Genesis 32:27-28 (AMPC)

Jacob the con man, always running from his enemies, was changed into Israel the favored, the victorious, the apple of God's eye. The woman at the well left behind her water pots, instantly becoming an evangelist to her entire town – perhaps she was even the very first evangelist. The insane man among the Gadarenes filled with a legion of demons begged to go with Jesus, but instead transformed into a powerful preacher, the first evangelist to the Gentiles in the Decapolis, the region of ten Greek cities.

The daughter of God who slung her dance bag into the dumpster pursued her business degree and now earns six figures, funding missions for the kingdom of God. What is your name?

The woman caught in the very act went away with dignity and sinned no more. The lame man from birth went away leaping for joy. Jairus' daughter died, but he received his daughter back to life. God, the One we must answer to, now asks, "What is your name?"

What is the fig leaf, the false identity that you picked up living in the course of this world, obscuring who you really are? Sanctification is the process of becoming more like Jesus, a work of the Holy Spirit within us that we follow by faith, empowered by His grace alone. Are we willing to lose the false identity assigned to us by the world? It takes courage, my friend – God-courage.

A dear friend of the ministry shared that at age 11, she was chased home from school by a group of about 20 high-school age girls who wanted to beat her up. Fortunately, she saw them coming first – and she ran through yards, jumping over fences, finally finding an empty doghouse to hide in as the girls pored through the neighborhood street by street, searching for her. When she saw the group pass by, she continued jumping through backyards until she arrived home safely.

The next day at school, she was teased and ostracized – until someone decided to stand up for her. Gabrielle Gibbs wasn't even the same color as her, but she told the entire group they better leave her cousin alone or she was going to "whoop" them all. No, they weren't cousins – but at that moment she was nothing less than the hand of God. Although she didn't get jumped, experiences like this can leave a root of rejection, making us vulnerable to Satanic influence and believing false things about our value and identity.

"When a Samaritan woman came to draw water, Jesus said to her, "Will you give me a drink?" (His disciples had gone into the town to buy food.) The Samaritan woman said to him, "You are a Jew and I am a Samaritan woman. How can you ask me for a drink?" (For Jews do not associate with Samaritans). Jesus answered her, "If you knew the gift of God and who it is that asks you for a drink, you would have asked him and he would have given you living water." "Sir," the woman said, "you have nothing to draw with and the well is deep. Where can you get this living water? Are you greater than our father Jacob, who gave us the well and drank from it himself, as did also his sons and his livestock?"

Jesus answered, "Everyone who drinks this water will be thirsty again, but whoever drinks the water I give them will never thirst. Indeed, the water I give them will become in them a spring of water welling up to eternal life." The woman said to him, "Sir, give me this water so that I won't get thirsty and have to keep coming here to draw water." He told her, "Go, call your husband and come back." "I have no husband," she replied. Jesus said to her, "You are right when you say you have no husband. The fact is, you have had five husbands, and the man you now have is not your husband. What you have just said is quite true."
John 4:7-17 (NIV)

Jesus knew she had no husband – His request was designed to spark a certain conversation. He is asking her, "What is your name?"

He wanted to talk with her about this lifestyle which did not reflect her true identity, but only her fallen, sin nature and the "bandaid" cover-up she was attempting to put on it.

Not just one, but five husbands had married her and then given her a bill of divorce. We don't know why, but can probably infer here that a root of rejection had taken hold, and she had given up on marriage; the man she was with now was not even her husband.

Jesus had the living water for her but He also longed to heal her broken condition. No longer would she be a wife rejected, inadequate and defective, but a beloved daughter, accepted and approved - destined to announce the arrival of the Messiah Jesus, the God-man, to her entire city.

Notice that Jesus did not condone her sin nor did He rub her nose in it by condemning her. She came to the place of truth within, and the Truth set her free (John 4:23-24; 8:32).

"Then, leaving her water jar, the woman went back to the town and said to the people, "Come, see a man who told me everything I ever did. Could this be the Messiah?" They came out of the town and made their way toward him."
John 4:28-30 (NIV)

You can come to God with gut-level honesty about who you've been and what you've done. In fact, that is exactly what He wants you to do! That's why the Bible says, "Lord, who may dwell in your sacred tent? Who may live on your holy mountain? The one whose walk is blameless, who does what is righteous, who speaks the truth from their heart;" (Psalm 15:1-2, NIV). He doesn't want you to pretend – He wants you to confess and renounce so that He can make all things new.

When you turn from sin to agree with Him, He makes all things new (2 Corinthians 5:17). He isn't going to kick you when you're down – He is going to embrace you, forgive you and cleanse you of all unrighteousness. In Christ, you are not what you have done, and you are not what people have said about you. You have the power to become who God created you to be - it all begins when you get alone and get honest with Jesus. He is there waiting for you - and your new, true identity is with Him. Remember, He essentially asks the Samaritan woman, "What is your name?" And then He changes it.

Remember the ultimate promise of God in Revelation 2:17: "Whoever has ears, let them hear what the Spirit says to the churches. To the one who is victorious, I will give some of the hidden manna. I will also give that person a white stone with a new name written on it, known only to the one who receives it."

What is the label that your siblings called you, your friends and schoolmates called you, maybe even your parents called you? Jacob, what is your name? Get ready to peel it off and leave it behind! The Word of God declares over you that "what you will be has not yet been made known."

"Dear friends, now we are children of God, and what we will be has not yet been made known. But we know that when Christ appears, we shall be like him, for we shall see him as he is."
1 John 3:2 (NIV)

Are you the next generation of preachers, teachers, evangelists, leaders of people to Christ? When you release the fig leaves to God, sling the dance bag in the trash, drop the waterpots at the well and run after Christ, what will you be? One thing we know for sure – you will be like Him.

"The Son is the radiance and only expression of the glory of our awesome God reflecting God's Shekinah glory, the Light-being, the brilliant light of the divine, and the exact representation and perfect imprint of His Father's essence, and upholding and maintaining and propelling all things [the entire physical and spiritual universe] by His powerful word [carrying the universe along to its predetermined goal]. When He [Himself and no other] had [by offering Himself on the cross as a sacrifice for sin] accomplished purification from sins and established our freedom from guilt, He sat down [revealing His completed work] at the right hand of the Majesty on high [revealing His Divine authority]"
Hebrews 1:3 (AMP)

You were created to reflect His light, carry His name, and be in His family – a carrier of His light and truth.

"But God, who is rich in mercy, because of His great love with which He loved us, even when we were dead in trespasses, made us alive together with Christ (by grace you have been saved), and raised us up together, and made us sit together in the heavenly places in Christ Jesus, that in the ages to come He might show the exceeding riches of His grace in His kindness toward us in Christ Jesus."
Ephesians 2:4-7 (NKJV)

You are not what the world says you are. You are not even what your family and friends say you are. You are who God says you are – and to walk in His light, we must release ourselves from every label, every weight and false pretense of the flesh so His light can shine.

Did you know our youth have rejected the standard of the past few decades? Statistics show that the key to reaching Generation Z (born between 1996 and 2010) is not by being perfect, but by being authentic. (Guan, 2024)

Our youth do not want your canned speeches, polished performances and slicked back hair. We were taught the value of preparation, of putting your best foot forward and looking the part, but something in our atmosphere has changed. Our youth crave authenticity; they long for the raw, unfiltered Jesus. They want to see Him flip tables, tell the Pharisees they are vipers, embrace the suffering and heal the sick. They won't go to your shows, dance your social dances or even smile at the cash register. Our youth need something real to hang on to, and we must deliver. Could they see end-times prophecy unfold?

Have you heard of the "Gen Z Stare"? The humorous phrase describes a neutral look by a 20-something-year old, often in a position of customer service, who reacts with a blank stare instead of enthusiasm. We value excellence and customer service highly, but let's unpack something here. Youth are rejecting the modus operandi of generations past. Even human resource professionals are taking notice: "Many Gen Z candidates reject the notion of "fake it till you make it." (Harper, 2025)

Let's ask ourselves honestly: are we seeing our youth reject a weakness of prior generations - an overemphasis on appearances?

A childhood friend used to brag that his dad ran the armory where the wrestlers were wrestling, and he used to get free tickets to wrestling shows for himself and all his friends. He enjoyed some prestige until one day, the neighborhood kids were all at his house, and his dad made mention of his job. It turns out that his dad was the janitor, which he was embarrassed about, but his grand lie only made things worse, and his friends never let him live it down.

When a person has not found his true worth and value in God, he or she learns to cope with insecurities by such things as projecting an image we want others to see. Our children see us lying and projecting, and they learn from our actions. How do we remove the mask we have carefully cultivated, coiffed and projected?

"Therefore, from now on, we regard no one according to the flesh. Even though we have known Christ according to the flesh, yet now we know Him thus no longer. Therefore, if anyone is in Christ, he is a new creation; old things have passed away; behold, all things have become new."
2 Corinthians 5:16-17, NKJV

What if we saw people not for their status, appearance and polite speech (or, not-so-polite speech) - but for their character, ability and God-given strengths? We can only walk in discernment of others and ourselves by truly walking by faith in the Son of God.

Have you ever heard the phrase, "If people weren't buying, others wouldn't be selling?" Maybe we need to stop being so impressed by surface things. If we stop buying the mask others are selling, we can reach the treasured person hiding inside.

"But if we walk in the light, as he is in the light, we have fellowship with one another, and the blood of Jesus his Son cleanses us from all sin."
1 John 1:7 (ESV)

Father, in the name of Jesus, thank You that I am complete in You. Thank You for breaking every iniquity and generational curse off of me and my family by the blood of Jesus. Thank you that I am grafted into Your family and Jesus' blood now runs through my veins. Thank you that I am the righteousness of God in Christ Jesus and accepted in the beloved. Please help me to get my fulfillment only from knowing that I have pleased You!

Give me Your vision to see others as You see them. Show me the treasure You have placed in earthen vessels. Your word says not to regard anyone according to the flesh, but to see people as You see them. Let me walk not according to appearances, but to boldly stand before others transparently, speaking Your truth in love, growing up into the measure, stature and fullness of Christ. Help me to walk in Your transparency and love, and release others around me to do the same.

Lord, help me and my family drop all fear and false pretense so that we can be exactly who You have called us to be in this earth. We know this flaw has kept us from reaching our children, and we want to change. We agree with You, God. Anoint us to show Jesus to those around us, and bring our children home to faith in You. Break fear off of every person reading this, and send out Your boldest, most authentic, wildest workers to reap the great harvest in Your fields of glory. In the name of Jesus we pray, Amen.

Chapter 6

The Two Trees

The Methuselah Tree is a closely guarded secret. Reported to be over 4,800 years old, this ancient bristlecone pine tree thrives somewhere in the Inyo National Forest in the state of California (Dodds, 2025). Its location is hidden to ensure no harm comes to it, but scientists took core samples in 1957, and they were used to date the tree. How does a tree grow so old? The bristlecone pine tree is an "extremophile" – a species that somehow thrives despite extreme heat, cold, and harsh conditions. Despite impressive size after 4,800 years, it actually grows very slowly. (USDA, 2011)

"These are the visions I saw while lying in bed: I looked, and there before me stood a tree in the middle of the land. Its height was enormous. The tree grew large and strong and its top touched the sky; it was visible to the ends of the earth. Its leaves were beautiful, its fruit abundant, and on it was food for all. Under it the wild animals found shelter, and the birds lived in its branches; from it every creature was fed."
Daniel 4:10-12 (NIV)

In Daniel 4, Nebuchadnezzar is detailing a dream for Daniel, and God provides the interpretation to Daniel. If we stop right here, we can glean the prophetic picture of a tree. The tree being described here is Nebuchadnezzar, and it represents his reign and his kingdom system: large, strong, beautiful, famous, abundant riches and food – under his kingdom, many people and families found shelter living there (its branches) and there was food for all.

Of course, we read in the next few verses of Daniel 4 that Nebuchadnezzar is about to be cut down; but we call your attention to the prophetic picture of the tree. A tree represents a kingdom - an organized system of rule and reign that includes a king, with a certain kind of power structure organized within it. A kingdom can be evil or it can be good.

A friend of the ministry shared that his beloved stepfather, who has now passed on, planted small trees in the front yard of his childhood home while he and his siblings were growing up. Now that his stepfather and a few siblings have passed away, the trees in the front yard – now large trees stretching across the sky, giving shade to the house - remind him of the times they had together.

Trees have to be planted from seeds and take time to grow, but once they do, they provide a network of oxygen, shade and shelter for birds and animals, and their root system stabilizes and enriches the soil.

At creation, God placed Adam and Eve in a beautiful garden of abundance, with many pre-existing trees bearing delicious fruit. Adam and Eve did not have to plant these trees - they just had to take care of them. They were given a kingdom they did not have to build, and a powerful reign based on delegated authority from God. Adam and Eve's original kingdom was based on God's sovereignty and their relationship to Him. After the fall, Adam and Eve's authority and reign was taken from them and they were transferred into a lesser kingdom – until the arrival of Jesus Christ the Messiah.

> *"'The Spirit of the Lord God is upon Me, Because the Lord has anointed Me To preach good tidings to the poor; He has sent Me to heal the brokenhearted, To proclaim liberty to the captives, And the opening of the prison to those who are bound; To proclaim the acceptable year of the Lord, And the day of vengeance of our God; To comfort all who mourn, To console those who mourn in Zion, To give them beauty for ashes, The oil of joy for mourning, The garment of praise for the spirit of heaviness; That they may be called trees of righteousness, The planting of the Lord, that He may be glorified."*
> Isaiah 61:1-3 (NKJV)

What a mission statement! The reign and the kingdom of God were given to Jesus. Jesus, in turn, delegated the rule and reign of His kingdom on earth to those who follow Him – the heirs of the promise.

His intention in the Garden and today remains the same - that you and I inherit the kingdom of God and become trees of righteousness. He gives us a kingdom that we did not have to build, and a powerful reign based on His delegated authority. The kingdom of God is near you!

Out of all the trees in the Garden of Eden, we only hear about two of them - the tree of life and the tree of knowledge of good and evil. We know that Adam and Eve were forbidden to eat the fruit from the tree of knowledge of good and evil, but there was no restriction on the tree of life yet.

Remember the prophetic picture of a tree – a kingdom system, with the reign and rule of a king and an organization of power and those who benefit from it. Adam and Eve had two kingdom systems to choose from – a kingdom of everlasting life, or a kingdom of the knowledge of good and evil, which would bring sin and death. In one bite, the system of sin and death, with Satanic powers at the helm, entered into the world and the bloodline of all humankind.

You and I arrived into this system of sin and death created by that tree, our blood flowing with DNA written with iniquity committed by those who came before us. What will we choose? Do we stay in the system of sin and death and fight forces older than time in our own strength, as some do? Or, do we turn to Jesus Christ and enter His kingdom system of life and power – becoming the very heirs of God? You and I must each choose what "tree" – what "kingdom" – to exist in, just like Adam and Eve did. Choose well!

Deuteronomy 30:19b declares "... I have set before you life and death, blessing and cursing; therefore choose life, that both you and your descendants may live;" (NKJV).

In order to continue the recovery process, it is necessary to go to the root of the tree of knowledge of good and evil. Eating from this tree brought all of mankind into the kingdom system of sin and death, with curses in operation. God already had a plan, but it involved a process.

I know we talked about the law earlier, but bear with me! God had to institute law to teach humankind three simple things: 1) God's holy standard for righteousness, 2) no one is able to meet God's holy standard, and 3) the promise of the Messiah Jesus, the God-man, who would descend from heaven, become a man in the flesh and pay the price for all sin once and for all, fulfilling the law and indwelling the believer by His Holy Spirit.

Many people trip and fall over these three simple ideas: they either don't believe God has a holy standard; or they believe that a person can follow God's holy standard if they try hard enough; or (worst of all) they do not believe Jesus has come in the flesh, died on the cross, has risen again to give us eternal life and the Holy Spirit to guide and lead us in victory.

God allowed mankind to beat its collective heads for thousands of years against these three simple lessons. Which one do you stumble on? We all have a "favorite."

Recall that in Lucifer's conspiracy to strip Adam and Eve of their Glory covering, he attempted to sow pride: "You will not die, but God knows in the day you eat of it, you will be like God". Satan appealed to the "self" or the carnal mind; that is, the "I me, and my"-centered thinking. Satan suggested to Eve and Adam that they could indeed do what God could do, without Him. (That is stumbling block #2 discussed earlier).

"Brethren, my heart's desire and prayer to God for Israel is that they may be saved. For I bear them witness that they have a zeal for God, but not according to knowledge. For they being ignorant of God's righteousness, and seeking to establish their own righteousness, have not submitted to the righteousness of God."
Romans 10:1-3 (NKJV)

Those who believe they can make it to heaven by their own good works are "seeking to prove their own righteousness", apart from God. That, my friends, is pride.

Satan tried to convince Adam and Eve that by eating the forbidden fruit, they would be like God (and would not need to submit to Him anymore). They wanted to be "like God" – but without God.

"Therefore the law was our tutor to bring us to Christ, that we might be justified by faith. But after faith has come, we are no longer under a tutor. For you are all sons of God through faith in Christ Jesus."
Galatians 3:24-26 (NKJV)

Before the arrival of Jesus Christ, God put mankind under an iron-clad school master – the Law (the first five books of the Bible in the Old Testament). The Law is like a 'tutor' that makes known God's standard for holiness, and by it, we experience the humbling fact that no one, not one person, can keep all of the 613 laws all of the time. The Law is the great equalizer – we have all fallen short; not one person can be justified or acquitted, for we are all under sin – except Jesus Christ, who was the physical embodiment of God's holiness. Society doesn't recognize this glaring fact, but God doesn't recognize man's hierarchies – He is no respecter of persons (Romans 2:11). Living according to Biblical truth means we stop pretending that societal hierarchies are recognized by God - great and small, we are all under sin. Every last one of us!

When Paul speaks of his life before receiving Christ in Romans 7:18-20, he declares that his condition was, "…the things I want to do, I cannot do them and the things I don't want to do, I do". He goes on to acknowledge that nothing good lived within his flesh. Jesus Himself validates this truth when He said, "Only God is good" in Mark 10:78 and Luke 18:19. Paul was subject, as we all are, to the system of sin and death. Another kingdom system is made available to us through the blood of Christ – the kingdom of God that Jesus refers to in the New Testament.

The Tree of Life also represents the Holy Spirit. Paul declares: "Live by the Spirit and you will not carry out the desires of the flesh because they oppose each other. If you are led by the Spirit, you are not under the Law" (Galatians 5:16-18). In Romans 8:2 we learn that, "...the law of the Spirit gives life and freedom...". This is why our Lord Jesus, as the Son of Man said, "I can do nothing from myself" in John 5:19, 30; 8:28). Jesus was filled by, led by and mantled by the Holy Spirit of Glory (Luke 4:1; John 1:32-33; 1 Peter 4:14).

Jesus was "tempted at all points, yet without sin" (Hebrews 4:15). In the Garden of Gethsemane, Jesus prayed to let this cup pass from Him, but nevertheless, not My will but Thy will be done.

Notice that when Jesus came to the earth, His choice in the Garden was life – giving us access to eternal life and replacing Adam and Eve's choice to release the system of sin and death. Earlier in His life, while in Galilee He said, "The flesh profits nothing, but the Spirit gives life". Jesus did not walk by the flesh, but according to the Holy Spirit. Remember that the apostle Paul instructed us, confessing, "I must die daily." We live opposite to our flesh and it may not make sense to the carnal mind sometimes – life in the Spirit is dying to "my way" (my will) and yielding to HIS way (will).

The keys to covering lie in the two trees in the midst of the Garden of Eden: the tree of Life and the Tree of knowledge of Good and Evil. One represents Life and the other death. Life is God's way or "Thy way". Death is my way. In the Lord's prayer we recall, "Thy will be done." Remember Jesus in the garden of Gethsemane? "Let this cup pass, nevertheless, not my will but Thy will be done".

Songs of the past such as, "I Did It My Way" and "I've Got to Be Me" reflect man's tendency to choose the "I, me and my" way, rather than God's way. These songs provoked standing ovations because they pander to self-centeredness or absorption, which "seems right to a man but leads to destruction or death" (Proverbs 14: 12).

You can live a life that "looks right" to polite society and still be heading straight to hell. That's why Matthew 7:13-14 (NKJV) says, "Enter by the narrow gate; for wide is the gate and broad is the way that leads to destruction, and there are many who go in by it. Because narrow is the gate and difficult is the way which leads to life, and there are few who find it."

When Adam and Eve chose to eat from the Tree of Knowledge of good and Evil, they set into motion a kingdom system of sin and death with Satan at the helm. No longer could they partake of a perfect life and all the benefits God intended them to have, and God banned them from the Garden of Eden so that they could not then eat from the Tree of Life in their sinful state and become unredeemable. God restored them to a relationship with Him, but the "I, me and my" – the selfish nature - remained prominent in their thinking and action.

In other words, Adam and Eve gained a measure of recovery through the animal skins in Genesis 3:21, but access to the Tree of Life was not permitted, because mankind would be "stuck" in their sinful state as an eternal being, and God, in His wisdom, already had a plan for the redemption of His beloved family.

"But when the set time had fully come, God sent his Son, born of a woman, born under the law, to redeem those under the law, that we might receive adoption to sonship."
Galatian 4:4-5 (NIV)

At the right time, God sent His Son Jesus, restoring the ability to enter the kingdom of God, experiencing the full encounter with His Holy Spirit, the Lord of Glory (1 Peter 4:14), who is available to all who would receive Jesus, the Son of God.

Chapter 7

Pursuit of Glory

"I have come in my Father's name, and you do not accept me; but if someone else comes in his own name, you will accept him. How can you believe since you accept glory from one another but do not seek the glory that comes from the only God?"
John 5:43-44 (NIV)

Jesus poses a striking question here: "How can you believe...but not seek the glory that comes from the only God?" For context, He is addressing the Pharisees – the spiritually-dead religious leaders. Preferring their powerful positions over Jesus, they tried to prove their own righteousness by exalting what they could do by themselves (or, their "works"), rather than submitting to God's righteousness (Romans 10:3). Relying on the power of their own flesh, the Pharisees added even more rules, thinking it made them more holy and enjoying forcing others to follow them also. In Matthew 23, Jesus makes it clear to us that we are to be diametrically opposed to this mentality. So what does Jesus' question above mean? Don't we all desire to achieve glory?

Let's examine Jesus' statement above so that our hearts are pointed in the right direction here.

I was at a church meeting with precious, well-meaning believers who love Jesus. My heart was grieved when someone made this statement about a ministry that had fallen: "I knew there was something off because all they sang about in the praise and worship was 'Show me your glory.'"

Do you think there could have been larger red flags indicating moral decay, other than the praise and worship extolling God's glory? Of course there were. It is my personal conviction that the body of Christ has an infection of false humility — a fear of being seen doing anything too big for God, fearing someone will ask, "Who do you think you are?" It's been said that "humility is not thinking less of yourself, but thinking about yourself less."

Like crabs in a crab trap that keep pulling each other down, we eventually become too afraid to crawl out of the box. Where are the believers who demand the God of Elijah?

"Jesus said to them, "My food is to do the will of Him who sent Me, and to finish His work. Do you not say, 'There are still four months and then comes the harvest'? Behold, I say to you, lift up your eyes and look at the fields, for they are already white for harvest! And he who reaps receives wages, and gathers fruit for eternal life, that both he who sows and he who reaps may rejoice together. For in this the saying is true: 'One sows and another reaps.' I sent you to reap that for which you have not labored; others have labored, and you have entered into their labors."
John 4:34-38 (NKJV)

Our "food", or fulfillment, is to do the will of the Father and to finish His work. Even more, other believers have labored, and Jesus will send us to step into their shoes and continue their work – whatever little bit might be left, and even to reap what they worked for. You just need to go stand where God leads you, do what He asks, and you will reap what He has pre-destined you to reap (Ephesians 1:11). Can we trust Jesus at His Word?

"You are the light of the world. A town built on a hill cannot be hidden. Neither do people light a lamp and put it under a bowl. Instead, they put it on its stand, and it gives light to everyone in the house. In the same way, let your light shine before others, that they may see your good deeds and glorify your Father in heaven."
Matthew 5:14-16 (NIV)

What do people do when they see your good deeds? They glorify your Father in heaven. Seeking the glory of God is a natural byproduct of authentic faith in Jesus Christ, and a basic teaching of Jesus. Don't back away now – I've only just gotten started stirring this pot.

What was Jesus getting at in John 5:43-44 above? We are all seeking glory from something. Yes, you are – even you. Either you will derive glory from people, striving to impress them with your charm, brains, attractiveness, strength, deeds, education, and accomplishments, using your works to project an image of who you think you have to be – these are the masks we talked about earlier.

OR, you will be seeking the glory of God, letting your light shine before others, blazing trails of signs following, so that all know that God is with you and He is glorified. Which one do you choose? Let's ask the Holy Spirit to help us remove the "fig leaves" and pursue His glory!

Many of us were brought up in a strict religiosity where any kind of rejoicing was dampened with a kind of false humility. We need to hold that up in the light of scripture – that kind of thinking can be a form of legalism. The Bible declares:

> *"...the people who know their God shall be strong, and carry out great exploits."*
> Daniel 11:32b (NKJV)

The phrase translated here as "shall be strong" is the Hebrew word, chazaq, which is a verb meaning, "to fasten upon; to seize, be strong and obstinate; to catch, bind, restrain, and conquer; to be of good courage and encourage one's own self; to be established, make hard, harden; to become mighty, prevail; to be recovered; to repair, retain, seize, to behave self valiantly, to withstand."

We can do nothing apart from Him, but don't forget the other half of that sentiment: If we are in Him and He is in us, we will bear much fruit (John 15:5). God's Word has released us like warriors into the battle of good and evil on earth - it is natural to desire great exploits for Him. Allow the Father to guide you by His Word and the Holy Spirit, and you only need to follow. The dance is between you and Jesus alone, but all will see and glorify Him.

Our Lord walked in humility. Three times He said, "I can do nothing from myself" (John 5: 19, 30; 8:28). He gave no opportunity for the flesh (I, me, my-centered actions and thinking). He said, "the flesh profits nothing" (John 6:63, NKJV). Jesus achieved the ultimate exploit and most glorious victory ever recorded – He lived a perfect, sinless life, offered His body as a sacrifice for the sins of the world, and was resurrected by the power of the Holy Spirit, and has ascended to sit on the right hand of the Father, where He forever lives to intercede for you and I.

Performance is the basis for all other world religions. Man's efforts to reach and find God's acceptance through works of righteousness are always, "I, me and my"-centered. No one can approach and find God through works and performance, or be made acceptable through self-effort. People might be impressed, but not God, the Holy One. Man cannot save himself. That is why Jesus is the Savior who rescues us from the power of sin, separation from God, and Hell that awaits all who reject God's way back into fellowship and relationship with Him through His Son, Jesus Christ. So, the Spirit of God, whom Peter calls, "the Lord of Glory" (I Peter 4:14), resided in and rested upon our Lord (Matthew 3:16; John 1:32-33).

Jesus' prayer in John 17:1 expresses His desire to honor Heavenly Father God through His obedience thereby reflecting His Glory. "Glorify Your Son that Your Son might Glorify You" (John 17:1). This was His motive and desire expressed; that we should walk in the glory He gave us, which He received from the Father:

"I do not pray for these alone, but also for those who will believe in Me through their word; that they all may be one, as You, Father, are in Me, and I in You; that they also may be one in Us, that the world may believe that You sent Me. And the glory which You gave Me I have given them, that they may be one just as We are one: I in them, and You in Me; that they may be made perfect in one, and that the world may know that You have sent Me, and have loved them as You have loved Me."
John 17:20-23 (NKJV)

Are we seeking the glory of man or are we seeking to glorify God? I have never heard a church go so quiet as when that question is asked. It is easy to fall into religion and condemn ourselves unnecessarily or belittle another believer's motivation for their good works.

Many times we consciously know when we are seeking to please man, or we become aware that our actions were to impress someone when we see the fruit afterwards isn't God's best. There are times we don't know our own or other's true motivations (whether seeking man's glory, or God's), and we can needlessly condemn ourselves or others. It's important to reserve judgment for Jesus to make the final call.

"If our hearts condemn us, we know that God is greater than our hearts, and he knows everything. Dear friends, if our hearts do not condemn us, we have confidence before God and receive from him anything we ask, because we keep his commands and do what pleases him. And this is his command: to believe in the name of his Son, Jesus Christ, and to love one another as he commanded us. The one who keeps God's commands lives in him, and he in them. And this is how we know that he lives in us: We know it by the Spirit he gave us."
1 John 3:20-24 (NIV)

Let's ask the Holy Spirit to reveal to us any places we are seeking the glory of man and give Him an invitation to lovingly prune those dead works from our lives.

When we are made aware of the hidden places where we are excessively seeking to impress or please other people, the Holy Spirit will bring to our remembrance that we need to take off these old ways, and die to self; that is, to crucify the "me, my, and I" self-centered way of living and thinking. We should be good to people, but we can't live to please and seek glory from people. We are created to seek after and reflect to others the glory of God!

By dying to self, we can appropriate the garments of glory that God has provided through Jesus and the Holy Spirit's presence in and upon us. This is what the apostle Paul refers to when he says, "I die daily" and "I am crucified with Christ". Remember that the Holy Spirit is the Lord of glory, (1 Peter 4:14).

When we accept Jesus Christ as our Savior and walk according to the guidance and promptings of the Holy Spirit, He is our glory covering. Will you come with Him on a new journey?

Chapter 8

Process of Glory

"For I consider that the sufferings of this present time are not worthy to be compared with the glory which shall be revealed in us. For the earnest expectation of the creation eagerly waits for the revealing of the sons of God."
Romans 8:18-19 (NKJV)

As we begin to consider the process of glory, let us consider one of the many Superman movies, Man of Steel. Whether you're familiar with the movie or not, the premise is that Superman arrives on earth, destined to save humanity and earth itself, but he struggles with loneliness, rejection and even awkwardness in learning to use his superhuman powers. The central focus is watching the main character, Superman, overcome and fulfill his destiny.

To make it personal, see yourself in Superman. View yourself as the main character who is waiting to be revealed to all of creation. Just as our Lord Jesus finished His work, now the body of Christ on earth, His church, is to carry out His plans and it starts with you and I as individuals in the process.

Like a movie watched with rapt attention, not only your Father in heaven, the Lord Jesus and all the angels, but all of creation are watching, eagerly waiting to see the revealing of the sons and daughters of God. Who are the children of God?

"Yet to all who did receive him, to those who believed in his name, he gave the right to become children of God— children born not of natural descent, nor of human decision or a husband's will, but born of God."
John 1:12-13 (NIV)

Now don't be disturbed because I like the Man of Steel. And let's keep our big picture straight: Jesus Christ is the main character. As we look to Him, He is the One we revolve our lives around. As we behold Him, as the Apostle Paul puts it, "we are changed or transformed from glory to glory with ever increasing glory that comes from Him." (2 Corinthians 3:18, NKJV)

We don't subscribe to the modern, "selfish" ideologies of the world by being overly focused on self, but let us not throw the baby out with the bathwater.

He created us – we did not create ourselves. We were lost, but He pursued us. We did not choose Him, but He chose us (John 15:16).

We didn't love Him first – otherwise, that would make us righteous, and the Bible says no one is righteous – not even one (Romans 3:10). We love Him because He first loved us.

"This is love: not that we loved God, but that he loved us and sent his Son as an atoning sacrifice for our sins. Dear friends, since God so loved us, we also ought to love one another."
1 John 4:10-11 (NIV)

We choose Him because He chooses us, and causes us to approach Him (Psalm 65:4). Let's not put the chicken before the egg – His incomparable love for us came first. He came, died and rose again – He has finished His work.

The time has come for His children to arise, and all of creation eagerly awaits.

So what does Romans 8:19 above mean? All of creation is waiting for you to overcome the betrayals, the pain, and the fear. All of creation is expecting the time to come when you walk in His gifts and reflect His glory.

Beloved, just like we watched Man of Steel, all of creation is watching for God's plot line to unfold– for the revealing of His glorious sons and daughters!

A dear friend of the ministry had a son who fought cancer three times. After his second bout with cancer around age 8, his left arm would not fully extend due to surgery for removal of cancer from bone in his arm. Our friend, being a good and wise father, placed his son in drum lessons, believing that would assist with the development and use of his left arm. After 8 years of practice, his son was so skilled, that his trainers commented his drumsticks had almost no "chew marks" on them – a mark of good form. Do you know how proud our friend was of his son? Our friend shared clips of his son playing the drums with anyone who would listen.

How much more delighted is our Father in heaven when we look to Jesus and walk out His plans?

At this point it is important to grasp that this is an ongoing process of choosing to walk in the Spirit, filled and clothed by Him. We choose to "put on" the armor of light (Roman 13:12); the Lord Jesus Christ (John 13:14); incorruption and immortality (I Corinthians 15:54); the new man (Ephesians 4:24); tender mercies, kindness, humility, meekness, long suffering (Colossians 3:12); the full armor of God (Ephesians 6:11) and love (Colossians 3:12, 14).

When God created you, He had an intention. He intended that you, like Jesus, "grow in wisdom and stature, and in favor with God and man" (Luke 2:52). How do we go through this process of glory?

Let me take the stress off right now – He does it. He leads, and we follow. He reveals a few steps, and then you take a few steps. The glory of God covers you as you follow in His steps of this predestined rhythm of your life, and becomes a beautiful, real-life movie to all around you who are watching.

Yes, people are watching your life! The Bible declares in Luke 8:16 (NIV): "No one lights a lamp and hides it in a clay jar or puts it under a bed. Instead, they put it on a stand, so that those who come in can see the light."

I've heard others say this, and it bears worth repeating: You are the only Bible that some people will ever read. As you follow Jesus, He is highlighting Himself to others in ways that you are not even aware.

Whether you know it or not, you are being watched by others - by God, by the angels, by all of creation - and they are cheering you on. All of creation watches with baited breath – eagerly desiring the revealing of the children of God.

> *"Therefore, since we are surrounded by such a great cloud of witnesses, let us throw off everything that hinders and the sin that so easily entangles. And let us run with perseverance the race marked out for us, fixing our eyes on Jesus, the pioneer and perfecter of faith."*
> Hebrews 12:1 – 2a (NIV)

How do we come back from where Adam and Eve left us? They ushered in a system of sin and death, but we walk in the spirit of life in Christ Jesus. When we choose to "put on" His armor of light and die daily to the flesh by His power, His supernatural process of change from the inside out restores us day by day. Stay in the process!

At the right time, God sent His Son, Jesus, conceived by the Holy Spirit and born of the virgin Mary. He is called the second Adam who was perfect without sin. He resisted what Adam and Eve succumbed to throughout His entire life as the Son of Man. From the Mount of Temptation to the Garden of Gethsemane, He maintained an obedient heart that said, "Not my will, but Thy will be done".

He alone was righteous before God without sin. We see God's plan of recovery continue at His baptism when He was immersed in the River Jordan. When He arose from the water, while He prayed, the heavens were opened, and the Holy Spirit descended upon Him.

The description is that the Spirit rested upon Him and remained without limitation. He was covered by the Spirit of Glory. Peter describes the Holy Spirit in I Peter 4:14 as "The Spirit of Glory".

Jesus wore this glory presence throughout His earthly life until His death on the cross where He paid a price to become sin, who knew no sin, that we might be made right.

Jesus the Anointed One brought back what Adam and Eve abdicated - the glory covering with authority and dominion - paving the way for our ultimate recovery.

The glory reflected on His countenance and His clothing as He prayed on the Mount of Transfiguration and as He walked on the water, when His disciples thought He was a ghost (John 17:5).

Throughout each day, we are faced with problems, circumstances and situations where we can choose to look to Jesus and follow the Spirit, or we can fulfill the lusts of the flesh. We need to answer Him, "THY will" rather than "my will".

We will encounter spiritual resistance. As Paul wrote to the Corinthians: "...the weapons of our warfare are not carnal, but mighty in God to the pulling down of strongholds, casting down arguments, imaginations, speculations, and every lofty thought raised up against the knowledge of Christ, bringing every thought into captivity to the obedience of Christ." (2 Corinthians 10:4-5, NKJV) When we submit to God, the devil must flee.

If you recall, James and John were affectionately called the "sons of thunder". In Luke 9:54, Jesus sent them into a Samaritan village to make preparations, where they were threatened and run out of town. They returned to the Lord, angrily asking, "Can we call fire down on them?". But Jesus replied, "You don't know what spirit you're of." When we are tested by what others do or say, we need to ask ourselves, "What spirit is this?"

We're transformed when we renew our minds in the Word of God. God's supernatural power in the scriptures interrupts negative and worldly thought patterns by adjusting the way we think to conform to the mind of Christ (Roman 12:2). We have the mind of Christ and we need to let HIS mind be operative in us by walking in the Spirit and faithful study of the scriptures so that our character is changed to reflect His nature (I Corinthians 2:16; Philippians 2:5).

When we experience God's manifest presence, we have an encounter with His glory, and we are changed or transformed. This can be best described as sensing a thickness or weightiness surrounding you. The glory of God is an awareness of who He is and what He does. This can happen in quiet times or in corporate gatherings.

This is what happened when Solomon's temple was being dedicated. The worship was unfolding and the glory cloud manifested, filling the temple so the priests could not perform their duties (2 Chronicles 5:13-14). Saul of Tarsus encountered the glory on the road to Tarsus and he fell to the ground when Jesus manifested His presence. The whole course of Saul's nature and life were dramatically changed (Acts 9:1-6). These are just a few examples of being changed with ever-increasing glory that comes from the Lord (2 Corinthians 3:16-18).

Remember our LORD admonished us to love our enemies and bless them. That's accomplished by dying daily to the flesh and yielding to the Spirit. When we walk in the Spirit, we do not fulfill the lusts of the flesh and the Glory of God manifests and rests upon us. In Christ our glory covering is restored!

Moses had numerous encounters with the God of glory. He was powerfully influenced when he drew near to a strange burning bush that, although burning, did not burn up – it was the glory of God. After time speaking with the Holy One, Moses' countenance shone with light.

Then there was Mt. Horeb. When Moses ascended to the height of this mountain, it became shrouded with a cloud of glory and flashes of light that terrified anyone who came near. Moses would also pitch a tent of meeting to spend time with God on a regular basis. The glory presence of Almighty God would surround the tent as Moses had intimate conversations with God. I believe that these many encounters caused him to say to God, "show me YOUR GLORY!" This led to a divine experience where his face shone like the sun with God's shekinah light (Exodus 34:29-30). This was only a taste of the radiance that would be seen on the face of Jesus about 1400 years later.

Moses went on to pray a prayer in Psalm 90. Verse 8 (AMP) states: "Our iniquities, our secret heart and its sin, which we would so like to conceal, even from ourselves, YOU have set them in the revealing light of YOUR countenance." In the light of His face, we become aware of our hidden thoughts, fears and transgressions.

Moses was aware of the need to be restored in His Light. Therefore, it was the reason for his prayer. He knew of God's transforming power and the relief and freedom it brings.

Consider how original photographs were developed in the past. When light passes through a camera's lens and hits a light-sensitive surface, it records the light's pattern and a negative "image" is captured through the flash of light. The negative image can only be transformed into a photograph using special chemicals in a darkroom (Chai, January). God wants to transform us in the "dark room" of the secret place, where we can encounter His light for ourselves.

In Isaiah chapter 6, the prophet Isaiah seems to be going through a time of self-inventory. It was in the year that King Uzziah died. Uzziah was a good king, but he made a major and serious transgression in the end of his reign. Have you ever done great on something, but then fouled something up at the end? This king ruined his legacy by going into the Holy Place and offering incense at the altar. This is something that only the priest could do with penalty of death. It was a well-known part of the law - his presumption led to an untimely death.

In verse 1, Isaiah sees the Lord in all of His glory and describes the scene: "...the seraphim were crying, "Holy, Holy, Holy...", ascribing unadulterated worship to the Holy One. Seeing God's holiness caused Isaiah to cry out, "Woe is me. I am a man of unclean lips in the midst of a people with unclean lips. I'm undone!"

During his time as a prophet, Isaiah levied many "woes" on the nation of Israel and his fellow countrymen. Isaiah saw the light of God, came into the light and the light entered into him. This is what caused him to cry out, "Woe is me! I am a man of unclean lips in the midst of a people with unclean lips. I'm undone!" Even a man set apart like Isaiah because aware of his faults and unseen sins in the light of God's countenance. Afterwards, because of his confession and agreement with God, his sin was removed by a coal from the altar that touched his lips. Isaiah was changed after he confessed his sin. Yes, even the prophet Isaiah!

When we behold God's holiness by looking to Jesus and by studying the Bible, we are made aware of His goodness. We see where we fall short of His nature and have the opportunity to confess and repent. In the same way, when we agree with Jesus Christ, He can replace our own shortcomings, sin and flaws.

"If we confess our sins, he is faithful and just and will forgive us our sins and purify us from all unrighteousness."
1 John 1:9 (NIV)

If we are still justifying ourselves by focusing on others, then we have the wrong perspective. There's an old adage that applies to seeing the sin in others and not necessarily in ourselves: "When you spot it, you got it!"

"And why do you look at the speck in your brother's eye, but do not consider the plank in your own eye? Or how can you say to your brother, 'Let me remove the speck from your eye'; and look, a plank is in your own eye? Hypocrite! First remove the plank from your own eye, and then you will see clearly to remove the speck from your brother's eye."
Matthew 7:3-5 (NKJV)

When we uncover others, we uncover ourselves. Years ago, I found that I was criticizing some people in the Body of Christ because of my perception of their actions, which may or may not have even been true. One day the Lord impressed upon me (here comes the Light shining on my heart) and said, "that's MY Body...and that's you, also." The Lord came to uncover my heart (sin). As I responded to Him and repented, I was transformed.

It isn't that dealing with sin in the body of Christ shouldn't be done – it was an adjustment in my own methods and not having a critical spirit.

"Dear brothers and sisters, if another believer is overcome by some sin, you who are godly should gently and humbly help that person back onto the right path. And be careful not to fall into the same temptation yourself. "
Galatians 6:1 (NLT)

We are called to confront believers living a lifestyle of sin, but our method matters. Does God want us to stand by and watch a brother or sister be destroyed by lifestyle sin? Of course not, but the goal is always repentance and reconciliation to God, if possible. If the brother or sister can be sweetly pierced by the Savior's love and brought back to Him, then they will be saved from death.

How do we address the wayward brother or sister without the salt of His grace and walking by His Spirit? We have to fall on the sword of His conviction first, and then we will see clearly to help our brother. Don't fear the "uncovering" of the Holy Spirit - God comes to heal you and bring you from glory to glory in Him, never to harm or shame you. His approach is always the best.

Transformation starts in the heart. A pure heart will speak words of life, forgiveness, and blessing. We can love others from a pure heart because He first loved us. He forgave and demonstrated His love while we were yet sinners and deserved no love or forgiveness. He restored our glory by giving us His own – we can do nothing of ourselves.

God's plan for us is the same as it always was for Adam and Eve – to have dominion and increase from glory to glory - because of our relationship to Him. By looking unto Jesus and following His Holy Spirit, we are restored day by day into His image by the process called sanctification.

As we look to Him, His light shines to those around us that we may not realize are watching. You were created to reflect God's light, and as a son or daughter of God, we declare over you that you will fulfill all of His good pleasure in the name of Jesus!

Chapter 9

Presence of Glory

*"The Son is the radiance of God's glory and the exact
representation of his being, sustaining all things by his
powerful word."*
Hebrews 1:3 (NIV)

Have you ever walked away from something that was
rightfully yours? We have all given up our right to be the
winner in an argument, paid for the car behind us in the
Starbucks line, or done other good things that cost us a
little. No matter the situation, paying the cost usually
doesn't feel good, but the end result benefiting another
person makes it worth it.

However, despite our personal sacrifices or good deeds,
none of us have ever met God's holy standard for
perfection. You might be loveable and you may have
sacrificed for others, but you are also a lawbreaker – and
so am I.

Why do you think James 2:10 (NIV) says this: "For
whoever keeps the whole law and yet stumbles at just one
point is guilty of breaking all of it."

We're entitled to some rewards, but we're also due for
some negative consequences - negative consequences
that include eternal separation from God in a horrible
place called "hell."

By contrast, Jesus lived an absolutely perfect, sinless life. He is the "God-man"; the embodiment of God's Word in the flesh (John 1). His very being and His every action perfectly fulfilled God's law and all of the prophecies about Him in the Old Testament once and for all.

Despite being tested in every way, He never once broke God's law and thereby never ate from the tree of the knowledge of good and evil. He walked in glory and power, serving others to bring healing, restoration and great joy. He was not only outwardly perfect; His character was and is perfect – He never used His glory and power for selfish side pursuits. At all times, He did only what He saw the Father do.

By His position as the Son of God and His incredible works on earth, He was rightfully entitled to unlimited honor and glory from the Father – on earth and in eternity. He is the King of Glory!

However, rather than claiming His due reward on earth, Jesus set His eyes on you and me. Seeing our position as lawbreakers eternally separated from God, He willingly went to the cross to take our punishment and pay for our sin so that we could receive His righteousness, His rewards and blessing, and be empowered to do great works by the power of the Holy Spirit.

That's why Galatians 3:13-14 (NIV) declares: "Christ redeemed us from the curse of the law by becoming a curse for us, for it is written: 'Cursed is everyone who is hung on a pole.' He redeemed us in order that the blessing given to Abraham might come to the Gentiles through Christ Jesus, so that by faith we might receive the promise of the Spirit."

Jesus gave us HIS glory, taking our shame. Have you made the trade yet?

When you observe the followers of God in the Bible – whether pre-law (Abraham), post-law (Moses), or after Jesus' first coming (the New Testament), what is the common theme? God's common theme throughout time is righteousness by faith (Hebrews 11).

"The word is near you; it is in your mouth and in your heart, that is, the message concerning faith that we proclaim: If you declare with your mouth, "Jesus is Lord," and believe in your heart that God raised Him from the dead, you will be saved. For it is with your heart that you believe and are justified, and it is with your mouth that you profess your faith and are saved."
Romans 10:8-10 (NIV)

I don't know about you, but I can't follow a list of 613 rules to daily perfection. I might drive the speed limit, but when it comes to God's holy law, I could break 36 laws before lunchtime, if left to my own devices.

But one thing I can do - I can look to Jesus. I can look to the Savior and imitate Him. I know He loves me and I can approach the loving Father through Him. I can ask the Father in Jesus' name for help, and He will manifest His Spirit within me and give me instructions and strength to help in time of need.

I can ask Him to reveal Christ's love and power in me to live a life that is pleasing to Him. In the same way, He will give you His glory! This is what happens when we receive Jesus Christ as Lord and Savior. Christ in us, the hope of glory!

When you follow Jesus, He will cause you, by the promptings of the Holy Spirit, to follow His law. That's why the Bible says in Romans 2:14-15 (AMP): "When Gentiles, who do not have the Law [since it was given only to Jews], do instinctively the things the Law requires [guided only by their conscience], they are a law to themselves, though they do not have the Law. They show that the essential requirements of the Law are written in their hearts…"

Remember that Jesus said, "Do not think that I have come to destroy the Law or the Prophets. I did not come to destroy but fulfill." Matthew 5:17 (NKJV). Jesus will put His law in your heart by faith as you develop your relationship with Him. He also declared:

"On two commandments hang all the Law and Prophets. They are, Love the Lord with all your heart, with all your soul and with all your mind. And the second is like it: You shall love your neighbor as yourself."
Matthew 22:38-40, NKJV

This scripture is the very heart of Jesus. He dwells in our hearts by faith (Ephesians 3:17) and He is love personified. The love of Jesus Christ is truly revealed in loving our neighbor as ourselves. This fulfills the whole law (Romans 13:9; Galatians 5:14; James 2:8).

Think of a baby bird hatching from an egg. How does a baby bird go from a liquid state to a living, breathing, fully-formed chick? The egg yolk contains enough protein, fat and vitamins to bring the baby bird to completion. The tiny cells rapidly grow, feeding on the yolk, developing into a fully-formed baby bird pecking its way out of the shell.

Similarly, the perfect sacrifice of Jesus provides everything we need to go from being a lawbreaker to a resurrected younger sister or brother of Jesus, radiating His glory. What He starts, He will finish by the power of the Holy Spirit at work in you.

"Grace and peace be multiplied to you in the knowledge of God and of Jesus our Lord, as His divine power has given to us all things that pertain to life and godliness, through the knowledge of Him who called us by glory and virtue..."
2 Peter 1:2-3 (NKJV)

When Solomon dedicated the first temple in II Chronicles 5-7, he calls a huge assembly to honor the Lord and worship Him. The glory of God filled the Temple so much that the priests were unable to function.

"The trumpeters and musicians joined in unison to give praise and thanks to the Lord. Accompanied by trumpets, cymbals and other instruments, the singers raised their voices in praise to the Lord and sang: 'He is good; his love endures forever.' Then the temple of the Lord was filled with the cloud, and the priests could not perform their service because of the cloud, for the glory of the Lord filled the temple of God."
2 Chronicles 5:13-14 (NIV)

We can draw a parallel between God's goodness and His glory. Where you see one, you see the other. As you may recall, God told Moses that His "goodness" or "glory" would pass by him in the cleft of the rock in Exodus 33:18-19 and 22, almost making the words interchangeable. We could go so far as to say that His goodness is His glory!

When Moses came down from the mountain with his life-changing encounter, his face shone with the glory. He put a veil over his face.

"But whenever anyone turns to the Lord, the veil is taken away. Now the Lord is the Spirit, and where the Spirit of the Lord is, there is freedom. And we all, who with unveiled faces contemplate the Lord's glory, are being transformed into his image with ever-increasing glory, which comes from the Lord, who is the Spirit."
2 Corinthians 3:16-18 (NIV)

This is a very important process. Moses put a veil over his face to keep Israel from looking upon it. Even to this day a veil remains over people's hearts when reading Old Testament law, but whenever anyone turns to Jesus, the veil is removed. As we behold Him, like a mirror we are changed (transformed) when we gaze into His word and spend time seeking His face.

God's goodness and character are what change us. The implication is that looking to Jesus is like looking in a mirror and then we reflect Him. We get perspective by looking into His Word and experiencing Him. As Romans 2:4 declares, His goodness leads us to repentance.

In Haggai 2:7-9, we are promised that "the future glory of this temple will be greater than that of the former." When we receive the Lord Jesus, the Holy Spirit comes to reside within us. We are His temple and His Spirit dwells within us. God promised that His glory in the latter temple (our bodies) would be greater! In I Peter 4:14, the Holy Spirit is again called the Spirit of Glory by Peter. In John 17:22, Jesus prayed, "and the glory which you have given me, I have given to them".

The goodness of God coincides with His glory. The Spirit of God is His glory, which is promised to us who believe and receive. His goodness within us to others brings Him glory!

In the Old Testament, God showed his intention for his people to be re-covered with his glory. In Isaiah 43:7, He declares: "Everyone who is called by My Name, whom I have created for my glory...". Our Lord Jesus prayed this in his high priestly petition to the Father about Himself as well all disciples who would follow. That's you and me! In John 17:5, He pleads, "...glorify thy son that thy son may glorify thee." He gives us His glory to serve others His goodness!

As we grow in the knowledge of Jesus, He changes our character to resemble His own. That doesn't mean He changes our personality – to the contrary, your authentic self shines brighter with the light of His presence! He created you uniquely from anyone else for a reason. He also gives you good works to do, changing other people's lives. Even if He has only asked you to smile at someone walking by, you are doing His work. As you allow Him to heal you and cleanse you of any shame, you will remove the masks acquired from living in the world because they simply won't fit any more. Your authentic self radiates with His light as you walk with Him, leaving no need to hide or project an image.

Our faith walk isn't a place of perfection - there will be seasons of trials and temptation, but God promises in Psalm 37:23-24, NKJV, "The steps of a good man are ordered by the Lord, And He delights in his way. Though he fall, he shall not be utterly cast down; For the Lord upholds him with His hand." You are well able to take the Promised Land that God has for you!

Your "yes" to God could mean life or death for someone else. As Jesus reveals the false labels assigned to you and you align and agree with Him, you will move from glory to glory in Him. He wants you to be aligned with His word, covered by His glory, and embracing your authentic self – not who people said you are, but who He really created you to be and fully in line with His Word. Without Him, I can do nothing, but in Him, all things are possible. Your sphere of influence contains people who need your real self in Christ. They need His glorious presence in your life to overflow and "spill over" onto them, changing their lives forever!

Everything you have ever experienced has brought you to this moment, and God is asking: Are you ready to leave the past and walk in to the future? Are you ready to be authentically you, removing the fig leaves and putting on the glory of God? Trust Him at His word and become a new creation!

"Therefore, if anyone is in Christ, he is a new creation; old things have passed away; behold, all things have become new."
2 Corinthians 5:7 (NKJV)

About the Authors

Barry and Jan Perez established Harvestime Ministries International in 1997 when God spoke that He was preparing His church for the end-time gathering of souls. Revivalist Barry Perez and his wife, Jan, have traveled all over the U.S. and the world spreading refreshing, revival, renewal and restoration to the church. Harvestime's mission is to equip and empower God's people to cultivate and operate in the supernatural.

Social Media:
Website: www.harvestimemin.com
Youtube: @PastorBarryPerez
Facebook: www.facebook.com/barryandjanperez
Email Inquiries: barry.harvestime@gmail.com

Bonney Rosas helps ministers of the gospel get their message to the ends of the earth. She provides content, publishing and editing services, in addition to being a writer and author.

Social Media:
Instagram: @Broses_Draft
Email Inquiries: brosespublishing@gmail.com